What All Children Want: *Structure*

Opulence Publishing

By

Sheryl L. Brown, LMFT

This book is lovingly dedicated to:

Shawn
Thank you for being my high priest, my best friend, my companion, my lover, my husband, Shawn Durelle Brown. Thank you for being part of my destiny.

Christine (Mother)
Thank you for constantly speaking words of life over me as I fulfill my purpose in life.

Gayle Claiborne
Thank you for endlessly listening to me during the process of reading this book. Meet a friend, but keep the old; some are silver, but you are definitely gold.

Candy Brooks
Special thanks to Candy Brooks for your insightful wisdom on purposeful thinking and meaningful conversation. Thank you for believing in Shawn and me.

Contents

Preface VI

Chapter 1
Why a Solid Foundation? 1

Chapter 2
Social-Emotional Impartations 13

Chapter 3
Establishing a Fine Line: Boundaries 25

Chapter 4
Vertical Relationship vs. Horizontal Relationship 39

Chapter 5
Public Social Grace 55

Chapter 6
Purposeful Thinking 81

Chapter 7
Emotional Stability and Support 95

Chapter 8
Honoring Your Role as a Parent 103

Chapter 9
Keeping Your Word 113

Chapter 10
Meaningful Conversation 123

Closing Words 133

References 135

About the Author 136

Preface

Children are the pride and joy of their parents. It is during this stage of life, parenthood, that parents take advantage of their bragging rights to boast about their children to all that will listen, related or not. "My son Tommy is only five and can read at a fourth-grade level." "My daughter Samanda was tested at her school today and they discovered she is a genius. I always knew she had it in her. It runs in the family, you know!" Can you blame them? Such joy comes over a parent when she actually witnesses her child make great strides socially, emotionally, physically, mentally, and morally in the world in which we live.

But what if Tommy, the little bookworm who can read at a fourth grade level, tells you to shut up not only at home, but also in public? What if that darling Samanda throws tantrums at the mall, Wal-Mart, at church, or at your exclusive women's club? Does Samanda's genius status excuse her from being out of control? The point is, as parents we sometimes focus more on the good rather than acknowledging, addressing, and correcting the bad. Sometimes recognizing the not-so-good side of your child does not always feel good, especially if it brings back memories of how you were as a child.

Am I telling you to stop boasting to others regarding your child's academic, athletic, and even heroic achievements? Of course not! You definitely have bragging rights. But what I am saying is, your child may have too much of one thing and not enough of another. In other words, your child may lack balance in her life. For example, Samanda may be an intellectual genius, but she is self-centered and lacks positive social skills. A balanced child is respectful, talented, mannerly, honest, intelligent, morally sound, giving, and joyful, just to name a few, all rolled up into one.

This proportional makeup (respectful, honest, giving, etc.) is the byproduct of a child being raised in a structured environment where purposeful words, exemplified behavior, love, boundaries, guidance, and correction are constantly being utilized to shape their inner image, thoughts, character, social, and emotional skills. Children would definitely not be the first to admit it, but they need structure to help bring balance and direction to their lives—both in the present and future.

During the course of reading this book, you will learn the difference between vertical versus horizontal relationships and the appropriate time to engage in each relationship; three foundational levels of socio-emotional development; the right words to speak over your child; teaching your child how to speak correctly over himself, disciplining in love and not in frustration; how to conduct meaningful conversation with your child; and much, much more!

My desire is that you will allow this book to challenge you to reconsider your role as a parent from being just an overseer, navigator, and protector, to a carpenter and gardener as well. As a licensed family and marriage therapist, I have learned from my own personal experiences and from past clients that if an individual correctly and consistently applies the principles and steps presented to her, she will see positive changes manifest in her life. So shall it be for you and your child if you take advantage of the nuggets being presented in this book and diligently put them to work. You will not only see a difference in your child, but you will also see a difference in yourself.

As you read this book, ponder on this analogue: When a family makes preparation for their long awaited trip, the father or mother will make sure the right fuel is contained in the gas tank for the long journey ahead. The wrong fuel, or even worse, putting water in the gas tank, can put a monkey wrench in the journey, therefore delaying the family from reaching their final destination. The right fuel can make a difference between a smooth journey or a rough journey. The same is true when it comes to your child. Parenthood is not an ordinary thing, but rather it is an adventure requiring you to invest, cultivate, and impart the right fuel or substance your child needs to be properly equipped for the journey ahead.

I see you as that parent wanting the best for your child and therefore willing to go the extra mile to make sure she becomes the best. Here we go with what all children want, STRUCTURE!

WHY A SOLID FOUNDATION?

A House Built on a Solid Foundation

What I believe is missing in the arena of parenthood is the untapped revelation in knowing that the inner image of child is far more important to invest in then the child's physical abilities (i.e., athletic, academic, musical, etc.). As parents we can get so caught up in enrolling our child in "outer stuff" (enrichment programs and extra curriculum activities such as dance lessons, soccer, karate, computer classes, and so on), all in an effort to enhance, discover, or reaffirm their physical abilities, which is the byproduct of their innate talents and gifts. We fail to realize it is the inner image that is the carrier of the gifts and talents residing on the inside of our child.

A child that is taught how to be more dependent on his inner image as opposed to his physical surroundings is far more balanced than a child that is taught to depend on his sensory mechanisms (touch, taste, sight, sound, and smell). Why? Total dependency on one's senses based on the situation at hand limits an individual from going beyond the norm in order to experience the impossibilities.

A little boy who lives in Durant, Oklahoma, was diagnosed with intellectual and developmental disabilities. Despite the physical, social, and mental oppositions attached to this disorder, his parents decided to invest more time cultivating his inner image rather than focusing on his developmental limitations. As a result, this child is now reading at his appropriate grade level (fourth). Not only is this child academically excelling in school, but he is also known for being humorous, loving, kind, and respectful towards others.

Well, let's get started! I mentioned earlier in the introduction that you as the parent (and let me also include the educators because of the long hours they have spent with your child) are not only the overseer, navigator, and the protector of your child, but also the carpenter and gardener. In this chapter I want to focus on the carpenter side of parenthood. A carpenter is one who is known for their ability to build and repair.

During the course of building a home or high-rise from the ground up, the initial process always requires that a foundation be established by pouring down cement before the carpenter can actually start building the frame of the building. Just like the foundation of a building supports everything that rests upon it, the same applies to the lives of our children. The initial foundation you lay down (through words, affections, modeling, and instructions) into your child's life must be sturdy enough to support the inner image existing on the inside your child. Why?

The inner image is like a distribution center where gifts, talents, academic performance, creative ideas, purpose, and dreams are stored until they are acknowledged and physically acted upon. While the gifts, talents, and creative ideas are being stored in your child's inner image, the inner image is drawing from the words spoken over the child. The inner image absorbs the substance contained in the words in order to reaffirm and support the existence of the talents and gifts dwelling on the inside of your child. So now I hope you can understand why your words and actions have such a strong impact on your child's development.

Children's images of themselves feed off the type of foundation that has been poured into their lives, therefore causing them to become the byproduct or the reflection of their parental image. I will never forget watching a documentary about a young man who was incarcerated for killing his mother. During his interview he stated his mother was very mean to him as a child and always expressed how he would never amount to anything. This young man's foundation was definitely based on hatred and cruelty. As a result, his inner image took hold of the appearance of the foundation laid down by his mother's words and actions, and his physical action (killing his mother) became the reflection of his inner image, which led to his being sentenced to life in prison. Words determine one's thoughts; thoughts determine one's actions; actions determine one's habits; habits determine one's character; and character determines one's destiny. Words are powerful! Look at it this way: Shaping a child's life is like taking clay and carefully molding it into an image that can be of good service to him, as opposed to bad.

A Strong Inner Image

Having a strong inner image is the key to being successful in every area of your life. Why? Because the real you is your inner image. How an individual talks, acts, thinks, and makes decisions is actually portraying the inner image existing on the inside of them. An individual's inner image is constantly being reaffirmed and even shaped by what enters into one's eye gate, ear gate, personal experiences, or experiences of others. So parents, it is vital that you be sensitive to what you expose your children to, because their little images are at your mercy. Here is an example of how love and respect can be cultivated into a child's image. Let's say a child sees his mother and father embracing each other, holding hands, or speaking kindly to each other. These acts model love, affection, and effective communication. Let's break this down. The observation of his parents holding hands or hugging each other has now entered into the child's eye gate. This means the child is consciously focusing on the positive behavior (affections) and words being displayed and verbalized by his parents.

This information is passed down to the subconscious, or what I like to call the federal express, which not only records the information (in this case the actions and words), but also delivers the "recorded" information to the conscience, becoming part of the child's belief system. Even if there is a disagreement between the parents that is handled gracefully or not, the child's thought process is still absorbing and processing the information to use as a reference point when similar situations arise and call for a response. This is what I call the "process." So what can you do to make sure that your child's inner image is honorable?

1. Be real about your inner image. Make sure you have an inner image that is worth being duplicated. Are you confident in passing down the same inner image you use to operate from in life? You can always tell whether your inner man is worth emulating or not by the following:

1. By how you treat others. Are you rude and condescending to those you come in contact with? Or are you respectful and uplifting?

2. By the words that come out of your mouth. Are the words being released from your mouth filled with doom and gloom? "I'm afraid!" or "Nothing good ever comes my way."

3. If you are insecure or self-centered.

4. If you are prideful and reluctant to accept constructive criticism from others.

5. If you are not a pursuer of dreams but rather settle for how life is.

6. If you are held captive by your past, therefore hindering you from living life to the fullest in the present. For example, this particular woman could never come to the point of forgiving herself because of what she had done in the past. She literally rejected my advice in regards to being able to forgive herself and letting go of the past as part of the healing process. She was adamant what she had done in the past was unforgivable. As a result, her relationship with her daughter and husband suffered tremendously. Her past became her plot in life because her inner image was being plagued by unforgiveness that was being reflected through her actions towards others.

2. Eliminate all disrupters. Disrupters are negative behaviors and responses (i.e., negativity, offensiveness, fearfulness, lying, guilt, etc.) that have gained entrance into an individual's inner image and not only masked the image, but also disrupted the flow between the inner image effectively releasing the gifts, talents, and unique abilities, and the physical actions receiving and fully implementing the gifts and talents to their maximum potential.

Have you ever heard the saying, "He was not at his best?" Well, disrupters prevent a person from being or doing their best. There was a man who was known for his awesome ability to teach. He was gifted for his ability to captivate his audience through his persona. However, this man could never reach his fullest potential because his inner image was being masked by his drug addiction. Rather than speaking in front of a massive number of people in a big auditorium, he was aimlessly roaming the streets getting high. The honorable image he had a right to was being consumed and dominated by a disrupter.

As I was reading this section of the book to my husband, he recalled an incident where a friend of his went to visit a friend who was babysitting his two-year-old son. To his friend's surprise, the father was sitting there with his son watching pornography as if it were a baseball game! How can this father ever expect his son to have an honorable image if his image is less than honorable as a result of pornography (the disrupter)? Like father, like son! You might be thinking, *Why is it so important to have a so-called honorable inner image?* Let me make it short and simple: How you are on the inside will determine what will be publicly displayed on the outside.

Many people today are walking around frustrated, shameful, depressed, and sadly to say, even in denial because their physical actions are reflecting their disrupter. As a result, they are prevented from not only being fully devoted, but from also not allowing their gifts, dreams, and talents the opportunity to reach their fullest potential. Parents, in order to be real with yourself, you have to look beyond yourself for the sake of your children. You can do this by analyzing and determining what actions and behaviors need to be removed in lieu of having an inner image that is worthy of duplication.

During this step I recommend you choose a close friend or family member who has your best interest at hand and will not sugarcoat things to make you feel good. Why? You may not be cognizant or you may not want to admit a disrupter is attacking your inner image and renovation needs to take place on the inside.

3. Replace old thoughts with new thoughts. Once you have discovered the disrupter that has masked your inner image, the next step is to replace old thoughts that support the disrupter with new ones. Here's how the process works. Let's say the disrupter in this case is fear. Fear has masked an individual's inner image; then over time it begins to dictate their thoughts. Eventually their thoughts begin to dictate their actions.

Dr. Caroline Leaf, in her book entitled *Who Switched Off My Brain? Controlling Toxic Thoughts and Emotions,* indicated that the mind and body are inherently linked and this connection begins with your thoughts. Thoughts can sway every decision, word, action, and physical reaction we make. Leaf also indicated that 80 percent of our physical, behavioral, and mental illness are related to our thoughts lives (Leaf, 2009).

A person who is fearful of someone or something will have what I call "pre-thoughts." Pre-thoughts are rehearsed plans or strategies that are conducted in an individual's mind on how to respond to a certain situation (or person) before the event actually occurs. In other words, everything is being played out in their mind before it actual becomes a reality. After a while this becomes an ongoing cycle. Situations arise, plans or strategies are rehearsed in the mind, then action—all of which is supporting the disrupter, which is fear.

By replacing old thoughts with new thoughts you alleviate the thoughts supporting the disrupter and you begin to focus on new thoughts that are in agreement with the new image you desire to have. New thoughts can be acquired by reading or hearing life-changing materials and messages or observing people who possess the behavior patterns you desire to have. Let me emphasize that renewing your mind is not a one-time deal, but it is an ongoing process. Old thoughts have the tendency to resurface, so do not entertain the thoughts, but rather immediately replace them with new ones.

4. Put thoughts into actions. Finally, this step involves your bringing to life the thoughts that support the new inner image you desire to manifest through your physical actions. An individual is constantly pondering on the desired image to the point that their inner image, thoughts, and actions are in sync. Let me put this all together by giving you a scenario of how each step works.

Step 1 and Step 2: Mary had a baby about six months ago. While on maternity leave, Mary began to do a self-inventory check to determine what areas in her life needed to be adjusted in order to be a good mother and role model for her daughter, Amy. As Mary diligently reflected on self, she painfully admitted her life had been consumed with anger stemming from her childhood. Mary remembered growing up and always seeing her mother angry but never knew the reason behind her mother's anger.

Mary was unaware this disrupter, anger, which masked her mother's inner image for years, had been passed down to her, the second generation, to carry on this emotional trait. Mary's anger issues had even spilled over into her place of employment to the point that she had been bypassed on several occasions for a supervisory position. Mary was totally frustrated because she recognized she had been gifted with strong leadership abilities that would be an asset to the organization, but she realized her anger had been her downfall. The disrupter, anger, had finally been exposed, so it was time to break away from its stronghold.

Step 3: Several months passed and Mary sedulously studied and listened to life-changing materials and messages that addressed her anger issues. She was constantly exposing her mind to powerful principles that would assist in eradicating the anger dwelling within her. Mary pondered on these principles, and eventually replaced her old thoughts that once validated the existence of anger in her life with new thoughts that now supported her new inner image, happiness.

Step 4: After hard work and diligence, Mary is a new person and her attitude on life has changed for the better. Things that use to make her angry no longer have the power to dictate to her thoughts and actions.

Reflections

Reflections

SOCIAL-EMOTIONAL IMPARTATIONS

Social-emotional patterns for adults are basically defined in childhood. These patterns are derived from what I call the social-emotional foundation which was laid down by the parents based on their upbringing and level of understanding of the importance of imparting appropriate and effective social and emotional skills into the life of their child or children. The foundation can be solid, semi-solid, or weak.

A solid foundation is groundwork that is socially and emotionally sound and able to provide the skills needed to govern a child's life in a productive manner. A semi-solid foundation is groundwork that is socially and emotionally borderline, meaning there are some usable skills (i.e., being respectful towards an adult figure), but there are other skills (i.e., anger outbursts in the classroom, etc.) that are in need of replacement. A weak foundation is simply that the groundwork is weak socially and emotionally and cannot provide adequate support a child needs to advance in society. Social-emotional skills imparted into a child at this foundation level are usually dysfunctional and considered unacceptable to society but viewed as normal in one's environment.

There was a little boy who was notorious for physically attacking his teachers, school bus drivers, and peers when he felt threatened or if he was being corrected for modeling poor conduct. To make matters worse, his behavior was not only approved but also encouraged by his grandparents, who were his caregivers. Wow! As a result, this little boy was constantly being expelled from school, therefore hindering his academic performance.

Note: Just because a child's social-emotional development was built on a weak foundation does not mean his social-emotional patterns are beyond change. Modifications of dysfunctional patterns can occur throughout an individual's life, but this is solely dependent upon their maturity level and the individual's willingness to make changes that will be beneficial to effectively functioning in society. With that being said, why is it crucial for your child to be socially-emotionally developed at an early age? Before I get into answering this question, let me define social-emotional development.

First of all, what is social development? Social development is the process of externally growing, developing, and establishing patterns resulting from an individual's interaction with others outside of self during the course of life. What is emotional development? Emotional development is learned internal responses (i.e., happy, sad, angry, etc.) that are displayed through one's actions as a result of a thought created by a past or present outside influence.

Let me get back to the question I asked at the beginning of this chapter. Why is it crucial for your child to be socially-emotionally developed at an early age?

1) From birth to five years of age children are always in exploration mode and eager to master developmental milestones. Case in point: When a baby first learns how to walk, the table, chair, or the hands and legs of their parents become a safety net which the child uses to maneuver himself around his surroundings in an effort to experience the newness of being able to walk on his own. This is so he can explore his environment without being held or carried from point A to point B.

2) From birth to age five, children's cognitive, linguistic, physical, social, and emotional skills excel more rapidly than any other time in life.

3) Appropriate and effective social-emotional skills contribute to the level of success or failure your child will experience in life. When a child is exposed to "sound" social-emotional skills, their ability to interact within their home environment is of a higher standard than a child that is less exposed to sound social-emotional skills. For instance, establishing friendships or expressing one's needs or wants in an appropriate manner.

However, a child's ability to interact within their environment is inappropriate and ineffective when they are constantly exposed to dysfunctional or less sound social-emotional skills. This causes the child to not only experience challenges or to be labeled as a challenge, but also to be stuck at a certain developmental stage because she failed.

4) Early exposure to social-emotional development helps children to respect both boundaries and adult figures. Here is an example of a child who did not receive sound social-emotional skills in the area of respecting authorities and boundaries. My husband and I were window shopping in one of the malls here in Georgia. We decided to step into one of the main department stores to admire the clothing items on sale. About ten minutes into our shopping adventure, I heard a child screaming at someone saying, "You are not my mother! You cannot tell me what to do!" Right at the entrance of the store a little boy was refusing to go into the store and was yelling at someone I assumed was his mother. I had to turn around to see what child had the nerve to be so disrespectful in public toward an adult.

Poor Mom; she stood there tightly gripping the basket with the look of frustration, anger, and humiliation. I quietly left my husband's side and strolled over to where the action was in an effort to assist this mother in resolving a seemingly hopeless situation. I casually introduced myself to the mother and told her my profession involves working with children. With all intention, I changed the position where the mother was standing from facing the child to having her back towards him. I wanted the mother's full attention without the interference of her son.

The little boy was in total shock and really did not know what to do because 1) I disrupted the power struggle he was having with his mom; 2) he was trying to figure out who I was; and, 3) he was definitely wondering what I was telling his mom. In the brief time I had, I created this invisible barrier between the mother and the son because I needed time to coach the mother on how to effectively operate in her role as a mother and adult in order to take control of the situation at hand. I also wanted the son to learn from this social-emotional development "moment" that he was the child and his role was to listen and to follow instructions accordingly.

I told the mom to not say a word to her son and to push the basket and not look back, and she did just that. She pushed the basket in the direction she wanted to go and did not look back at all. The little boy looked at me; then he ran after his mother. Both resumed to their designated roles; the mother was leading and the child, of course, was following.

My husband and I laughed as we watched the little boy trying to catch up with his mother who was pushing the basket beyond the speed limit of the department store. I hope you can see the importance of children learning social-emotional skills at an early age. It is these appropriate and effective skills that will teach them to respect boundaries and authorities.

5) Finally, the fifth reason is what I call the "purest thought process" and is why it is important for children to learn social-emotional skills at an early age. The purest thought process is a child's conscious, subconscious, and conscience at its purest form and is therefore open and receptive to receive information being presented to it, which in turn forms the child's belief system. What is introduced to the child's ear gate, eye gate, and what the child actually experiences, either good or bad, determines how a child will view and respond to life. In other words, a child, your child, only knows what to think and how to respond based on what they have been taught or consistently exposed to.

Basically, your thoughts, beliefs, and attitude become the standard or norm that is passed down to your child. For example, Samuel's mother deeply disliked another race and made racial comments in front of Samuel, both in public and in private. Samuel was only three and had no clue what his mother was doing was wrong. Regardless, her dislike for another race was being transported. Once it had reached its destination, prejudice became embedded into Samuel's belief system.

Children are not born prejudiced, but rather words and actions that convey prejudice are constantly being presented to the children's thought processes until they eventually become part of their belief system.

The Open Window of Opportunity

I can never forget when it can time for me to pay the initial installment for the first run of my book, *Push: How to Birth Your Dream into Reality*. My bank declined the charges because the amount exceeded the limit I was able to withdraw. As a result, the printing company called me to explain that they could not proceed any further until they received the first installment. So I immediately called the bank to investigate this matter because I knew I had the funds in the bank to cover the printing cost.

I explained my concerns to the customer service representative and wanted to know how this matter could be rectified. The representative was given the authorization to grant me an open window, which was a certain time frame. This allowed the printing company to retrieve money from my account without any interference. I used this example to convey to you that there is an open window of opportunity or a certain time frame, in this case from birth to five, in which the thought process of your child is at its purest state and ready to absorb like a sponge any and all information presented to it.

Imagine the open window as being like a stage curtain for their life. The actors and actresses are parents, aunts, uncles, godparents, and teachers (whom I call responsible figures) who are performing for the first time before this sensitive audience. Their actions show how to love, establish friendships, how to communicate their needs and wants in an appropriate manner, how to resolve problems, how to be respectful towards others, and how to control one's emotions rather than letting emotions be in control. All of these are social-emotional etiquettes of life.

But what if one of the performers did just the opposite of what was written in the script? Rather than communicating his needs in an appropriate manner he would have a tantrum because he could not get his way. Rather than be pleasant towards others, the actor was rude and inconsiderate. If these scenes are not redone correctly, the audience will walk away believing this is how they should conduct themselves in life.

Sadly, there are a lot of children out there whose initial exposure to life is bleak. They are socially and emotionally deprived because the actors and actresses in their life were deprived themselves. As a result, dysfunctional behaviors are being passed down from one generation to the next.

I am reminded of story about a little boy who from the time he was an infant up to the age of six was exposed to his father physically abusing his mother. The father eventually left the home, but the stains of violence, anger, and disrespect were still left behind and were dictating the social and emotional skills that existed in this home environment, therefore distorting the child's belief system. The distortion in his belief system caused him to become the perpetrator, and his mother and his school peers were the victims. He became what I call an "imitator of his father" because this generational transfer had a carrier, the little boy, to spread this dysfunctional behavior.

Let me make something very clear before you think after reading this book, *If my child is not socially-emotionally sound by the age of five, I am a failure and there is no hope for him.* Please don't take your mind there! That is definitely not the message I am trying to send. Nor am I saying from birth to age five are magical years. But what I am saying, from birth to age five are "prime" years, priceless moments in which you as a parent have the strongest influence when it comes to imparting sound values, morals, social, and emotional skills.

Children are highly dependent from birth to age five and less dependent as they enter into mainstream school. Think about it; you are the one who tells them what to think, what to say, and how to respond based on the situation at hand. You are the one providing everything pertinent to the development and success of your child without the influence of the outside world. In other words, your child is depending on you to lead them on the right path so their journey in life will be meaningful and prosperous in every arena.

What am I saying is, there will always be windows of opportunities after the age of five to undo and replace your child with sound, social-emotional skills they may not have received or grasped during those prime years. But the process may take a little more work, because reprogramming the thought process of your child by introducing and replacing dysfunctional behavior with functional ones will need more than you telling him what to do or think. There also has to be a willingness to change on behalf of the child, especially as he becomes more independent and set in his ways as time goes on.

Your Social-Emotional Responsibility to Your Child

I hope by now you are convinced how vital your role is as a carpenter when it comes to the social and emotional health of your child. It is your responsibility—not the teacher's or any other adult figures—to be actively involved in laying down a solid foundation that socially-emotionally equips your child for the life journey ahead.

I would highly recommend that you reassess your social-emotional well-being to determine if what you are modeling before your child is worth duplicating. Why? In essence you are duplicating another you, so if the big you is socially or emotionally dysfunctional, then the chances are your little one will mostly likely be social and emotionally dysfunctional as well.

This observational statement I just made does not apply to all children. The simple fact is, there are some children who are fortunate enough to take after the parent whose social-emotional skills are strongly developed and adaptable to life.

Here is a list of activities that will require you to get involved in the social-emotional development of your child:

1. Have a story and music time. Find books and songs promoting self-awareness, establishing relationships, understanding boundaries, empathy, and understanding one's emotions and feelings.

2. Utilize daily activities. Utilizing daily activities (i.e., brushing teeth, getting dressed, snack time, nap time, etc.) as a learning tool that invites social skills into the arena of your home environment.

3. Model behaviors, both in public and private, supporting the social-emotional well-being of your child. For instance, let your child see you greet family and friends with a hug. Or let your child witness you taking care of business at the bank and being courteous to the cashier.

4. Incorporate "dinnertime chat." Let this family time be the highlight of the day. Communication plays a big part in the social-emotional development of a child. Dinnertime chat is time to teach your child the etiquettes of communication (i.e., saying "Excuse me" when others are talking, giving eye contact to the person you want to talk to (every culture is different). Parents, guide the conversation and interject as needed.

Allow your child to express what is on their mind without them feeling like what they have to say is insignificant. Let there be laughter at your dinner table. Laughter is medicine for the soul and body. Finally, always end with a recap of what was discussed during the dinnertime chat, and if there is a lesson to be learned, let it be told. That is why it is crucial as a parent to reassess your own social-emotional skills in an effort to determine if the social-emotional skills are appropriate for your child to emulate.

ESTABLISHING A FINE LINE: BOUNDARIES

Warning! This is chapter on boundaries is going to be brief and to the point, so pay close attention. Just like when you are getting ready to pass through a small town, you better not blink or you are going to miss it. In this chapter I want to get you to see another perspective on boundaries from the standpoint that boundaries not only separate and validate the roles of those who exist in a family system, but boundaries also assist in providing what I call "instructional space" for the parent to effectively instruct and lead and for the child to effectively learn and follow.

I will go into further detail regarding "instructional space" later on in this chapter. You will also discover after reading this chapter that boundaries are just one of many threads holding the family system together. It is during my counseling sessions with a family where I pay close attention to their existing boundaries and utilize my findings as a measuring tool which allows me to determine the strengths and weaknesses of the family based on their verbal and nonverbal communication or body language.

Personally, I believe the lack of or the weakening of boundaries between the parent and child have seemingly become more prominent over the last ten years for the following reasons:

1) More and more parents, not all, view their child as their best friend rather than their son or daughter.

2) Rather than correcting their behavior, parents are allowing their child to be physically aggressive towards them, both in public and in private.

3) There are little or no consequences for the child's negative behavior, only leaving the child to assume his behavior is acceptable when in actuality it is not.

4) Sadly, many children are left to fend for themselves as their parent indulges in addictive behaviors that require their full attention more than attending to and taking full responsibility for the safety and well-being of their child. As a result, the child is "parentified" (Thrust into a role that an adult usually occupies) involuntarily.

5) The divorce rate is constantly on an uprise. Parents are emotionally at war with each other, which oftentimes causes the child to be stuck right in the midst of the battle. This leaves the child to decide which parent they will be the most loyal to.

Finally, I believe the strongest contribution that boundaries can make to the family is that they provide structure and allow the family to operate effectively as a system. Now, let's takes all that has been presented to you thus far and elaborate more in detail.

The Significance of Boundaries

It is one's understanding of the true purpose for which boundaries were created that allows (requires) members of the family to respect boundaries and operate accordingly. Let's briefly look at the different ways boundaries serve in the family system.

Separates

Boundaries are designed to serve the family unit by separating the roles of each member of the family into their own entity. Each existing role within the family system should be independent of each other so each individual can be effective at what he was created to do. Boundaries strategically separate the roles making up a family system so each person can visually recognize, understand, and respect the function of each designated role accordingly.

For instance, it is so important for the child, especially the male child, to see his father function in his roles as a leader, provider, husband, father, and caregiver. Through observation the child is given the opportunity to recognize, understand, and respect the role of his father and to emulate his father once he has his own family.

Even though there are separate entities within the family structure, there is still a common denominator maintaining unification within the system. The role of the mother has its own entity or is independent of the role of the daughter. However, the common denominator between the roles of the mother and daughter is love, trust, respect, and attentive listening, all of which I consider as "active ingredients" needed to maintain unification between the mother and the daughter.

Validate

Boundaries bring validation to each member of the family. Each member must not only feel their existence brings meaning to the family, but also that their contribution to the family is of importance. For instance, it is extremely important for the wife to validate her husband for his leadership abilities and his dedication to the family. The validation the husband receives from his wife confirms his role in the family and that his contribution has not gone unnoticed.

The same applies to your child. They need to be celebrated, and their presence needs be constantly acknowledge by frequently expressing to your child that their existence in the family is priceless. A statement like "I am so glad your father and I had you; you bring so much joy to the family." This simple statement can make a world of difference to a child. Adding value to your child and to any member in your household through words and actions strengthens the family system. Always remember, giving your child a sense of belonging is one of the highest forms of validation a child can receive from their parents.

Instructional Space

Boundaries create what I call an "instructional space" so that impartation of information, wisdom, and demonstrating principles can be properly and effectively filtered down either verbally or nonverbally from parent to child. In other words, it is an environment conducive for teaching. When boundaries are properly in place, both the parent and child can get the most out of each teachable moment that occurs between them. How can a child learn if they are never properly taught?

The first institution a child is exposed to is their home. The child's first teacher in life is their parents. Oftentimes boundaries are so unidentifiable that when a teachable moment presents itself it is denied the opportunity to properly release the capsule of information it contains. This capsule of information has the ability to promote growth, understanding, and guidance in the life of a child. From past observations, children who are either parentified or treated like a peer by their parents are primarily operating from a system where boundaries are entangled, therefore causing the instructional space to be nonexistent.

What do I mean by parentified? When childhood pleasures such as playing with dolls or playing outside with friends are minimal or forfeited altogether for the sake of involuntarily becoming the caregiver for oneself or one's siblings (usually younger siblings). I can recall a story of a little girl who was seven years old and was left to care for her six-month-old sister while her mother went out for long periods of time. When the mother returned, if she felt the child neglected her baby sister in any way (i.e., the diaper was not changed or the baby was crying) she physically abused the seven-year-old. That was truly a severe case of involuntary parentification. This little girl was eventually removed from the home and custody was given to the fraternal grandmother.

Let me clarify myself before you get offended. I am not saying your child is being parentified if he helps you to change one of his sibling's diapers or has to babysit his younger siblings while you run an errand. However, what I am saying is if your child is totally being deprived or cheated out of his childhood pleasures in the process of alleviating you from your parental responsibilities, then I say your child is parentified.

Another destroyer of the instructional space is treating your child as if he were an adult. When a parent shares personal business with the child or asks his opinion regarding an adult matter, the parent is placing the child in what I call "the midst of an adult affair." Any child who is in the midst of an adult affair is being transitioned prematurely into adulthood. This premature transition into adulthood is not the best thing in the world because the child is more apt to become rebellious and even disrespectful in the long run.

This can be a nightmare for some parents because on one hand the child is trying to remain on his adult pedestal. On the other hand the parent is desperately trying to snatch the pedestal from underneath him in order for him to listen, learn, and obey like a child. For many parents this nightmare can be enduring due to the fact that the child has become comfortable with being in the midst of adult affairs or has embraced the role of an adult to the point that they see no reason why they have to return back into the world of a child.

That is why I place heavy emphasis on treating a child like a child head-on and avoiding exposing him to "adult" responsibilities, decisions, activities, or conversations that will remove him from the realm of thinking like a child and propelling him into the realm of thinking like an adult. A child has his place just like an adult has their place.

In a very small town there was an eight-year-old boy who was going on thirty. He truly believed rules did not apply to him and as result he did what he pleased. It all started when his father went to prison and left his son to be the man of the house. The father failed to instruct his son to listen to his mother. Because of this the little boy took advantage of his mother's gentle and kind spirit by being noncompliant.

The mother had other children to attend to and was becoming frustrated with her son because he did not want to be a child but wanted to be an adult. Rather than helping with household chores and going to school, he chose to take off on his bike and roam the streets of their small, remote town way into the late-night hours. This child's estimation of himself was that he was superior to his mother, all because his father placed him in the midst of adult affairs.

This totally minimized his opportunity to experience any teachable moments he could have had with his mother because the instructional space was never properly activated within this family system. That is so sad, because there is so much a son can learn from his mother that will be beneficial to him in his adult years.

Finally, I believe the strongest contribution boundaries make to a family is that boundaries support structure. Structure within the confinement of healthy boundaries brings order and allows the family to operate effectively as a whole. I believe a family system is at its best when it operates from structure. Each member of the family knows what to do, when to do it, and how to do it at the appropriate time because solid principles have been set in place.

Structure gives life to patterns, which allows the family to operate at the fullest potential in which it was designed. Therefore, the love, respect, support, and growth harmoniously flow within the family system. This helps to overcome challenges in order to maintain the social, mental, emotional, physical, and for many, the spiritual well-being of the family.

Taking Steps to Establish Boundaries

OK, we are coming to the conclusion of this chapter. Before I conclude I would like to leave you with five steps to assist you in either establishing or reestablishing boundaries that will strengthen and solidify the family system.

Step 1: Identify Existing Boundaries

This step requires you to identify existing boundaries in order to determine which boundaries serve as a liability or asset to the family system, especially the existing boundary between you and your child.

What is the difference between strong and weak boundaries? Boundaries are strong when you, the parent, value your role and it is quite evident through the love, support, guidance, and correction you provide to your child. Boundaries are strong when you, the parent, are familiar with the current boundaries existing between you and your child and you are also aware of the rules that make up a boundary or boundaries.

Oh, did you not know that boundaries are made up of rules? Well they are! For example, there is a boundary that represents the rule of a child saying "Excuse me" when you are talking to another adult. Boundaries are strong when both you and your child make every effort to adhere to the rules that determine the boundaries and recognize when one or both have stepped over the boundary line.

You have to teach your child at an early age to respect boundaries and constantly groom him until it becomes a natural response. You will be able to tell when your child is cognitively mature because he will make the necessary adjustments that will demonstrate his ability to recognize all boundaries applying to him. This includes being respectful towards you and honoring your position of authority, both verbally and nonverbally, as well as in public and in private.

How can you tell when a boundary is weak or nonexistent within the family system? When a boundary that is set in place is not being acknowledged by all those it is intended for. This causes the boundary to have no validity within the family system. I call this a one-sided effort. The lack of participation from one member of the family can weaken a boundary and hinder it from serving the family as a whole to the fullest extent.

For example, Mary, the mother and participating member, is frustrated but consistent in taking away Calvin's (the son and nonparticipating member) enjoyable activities and games if he does not do what she tells him to do (i.e., clean up his room). Calvin appears hurt when he has to suffer the consequences for his actions, but resumes his old behavior patterns after a couple of days. Granted, this boundary has the potential of being strong but will remain weak until Calvin is on board by adhering to his mother's requests.

Another way a boundary can be identified as being weak or nonexistent is when parents allow their children to do what they want to do, when they want to do it, without any rules to assist in monitoring and redirecting the children's behavior, in addition to setting limits to what they can and cannot do. Talking back to his parents, staying up all hours of the night watching television after being told to go to bed, parents not following through in implementing consequences to confront unacceptable behavior and disobedience, just to name a few, are concrete reasons that would cause me to conclude boundaries are either unidentifiable or weak.

Step 2: Modify/Replace

This step requires you to modify or replace rules that poorly represent the boundary. Always remember that a boundary is only as strong as the rules making up the boundary. The existence of a boundary hinges on the establishment of rules. In other words, the rules are the backbone of the boundary.

Just like the fence post is the support for a fence, rules are the support for boundaries. Boundaries must be supported by rules in order for structure to be effectively implemented within the family system. So if you are not getting the results you desire, you may need to modify or replace certain rules that are working for your existing boundary. Asking yourself the following questions will assist you in determining which rules should be modified or replaced:

1. Who is dishonoring the rules: the adult, child, or both?

2. When are the rules being dishonored the most?

3. Why are the rules being dishonored?

4. What are the negative outcomes for not honoring the rules?

Once you have answered these questions, two separate meetings are in order. The first meeting is the executive meeting. This meeting consists of the leaders of the family unit coming together to discuss and determine which rules need to be modified or replaced. Let's use our previous example regarding saying "Excuse me," but this time with a different scenario.

Kendall always interrupts her parents when they are either talking to each other or when they are conversing with another adult. If Kendall does not get an immediate response from her parents, she breaks out in a tantrum. This has become so embarrassing to the parents, especially when they are out in public. Both Tim and Leslie (parents) recognize Kendall is not respecting the rule of saying "Excuse me" before being acknowledged by her parents, therefore causing the boundary that exists between them and Kendall to be unstable.

Both Tim and Leslie decided it was time to have an executive meeting to determine what could be done to address Kendall's negative behavior. During the meeting they decided Kendall would still have to say "Excuse me" when wanting to be acknowledged by them. But they also agreed to verbally (both in public and in private) remind Kendall that she must say "Excuse me" if she wants to be heard by either one of them.

If Kendall has a tantrum, they will either ignore her and proceed talking or pick up Kendall in the midst of her tantrum and take her to a quiet place and let her know her negative behavior will not be tolerated. Tim and Leslie also decided there have to be some consequences for Kendall's disruptive behavior. So for every tantrum Kendall displays in public or in private, she will lose privileges by not being able to play with her dolls or playing with her friends.

The second meeting is between parent and child, or what I call the general meeting. This is where the rules and the plan of implementation are presented to everyone involved. Depending on the age of your child, role-playing can be an effective tool in order to demonstrate how the rule works and the consequences for not abiding by the rule.

Step 3: Getting a clear understanding of the new rule.

The social and emotional success of a family depends upon the family clearly understanding the rules that specifically define the boundary in which each member should operate within. Being able to answer the following questions will help you to determine if all members of the family properly understand the rule:

1. What is the purpose of the rule?
2. What is each family member's part in successfully implementing the rule?
3. What can we expect as a family if this rule is adhered to on a consistent basis?

For instance, a household rule may be when your teenage son goes out to the movies with his friends and is expected to call you when he arrives to the theater and when he is returning home. The clarification process is at its best when both you and your son recognize that the reason for this rule is to maintain communication of your son's whereabouts, reinforce safety, and maintain respect and consideration for those in authority over his well-being.

Now, when both you and your son are in one accord regarding this rule and its purpose, then the boundary supported by the rule is able to do what it was created to do, provide structure. I would definitely encourage you to have a family meeting to discuss the new rule, the impact it will have on the family, and demonstrate (i.e., through role-playing, etc.) how the rule should be properly implemented when needed.

Step 4. Putting the rule into operation.

Now you should be ready to put the new rule into action so all those it pertains to can acknowledge the boundary. Consistency is a must when implementing a rule, so if someone in the family is not following the rule exactly how you plan or want, be patient; he or she will eventually conform. Remember, Rome was not built in a day! Before you know it, there will be that harmonious flow from the parent to the child and from the child to the parent. Why? The boundary is properly set in place and the rules are sturdy enough to hold it up.

Reflections

Reflections

VERTICAL RELATIONSHIP VS. HORIZONTAL RELATIONSHIP

We as parents were created to be overseers of our children. An overseer does just that: sees over whatever or whomever she is in charge of. As parents we wear many hats during the course of parenthood (i.e., nurturer, provider, transporter, etc.). This particular hat we wear as an overseer requires you and me to be strong and firm, yet loving. This certain type of hat requires you and me to be cognizant of what is going on inside and outside of our home environment, keeping our children out of harm's way. You are the overseer of your child's health, making sure he eats right and stays active, in addition to taking him to the doctor and dentist for his regular checkups.

However, there is one aspect of the overseer I want to place heavy emphasis on. That is being the corrector or disciplinarian of your child's social conduct towards you and those she comes into contact with. Can I make it plain? There is nothing worse than a rude, disrespectful, noncompliant, selfish, uncontrollable child. This type of child makes teachers, relatives, the grocery store clerk, and even the neighbor's dog hate to see her coming and definitely elated to see her go.

Believe me, there are children out there just as I have described. These children did not become like this overnight; nor did they become this way on their own. They had help from their parents who either allowed their children to get away with things that should have been nipped in the bud early on, or the parents just did not know how to properly address their child's negative behavior.

Well, saying no would have been a good start. "I don't want little Blake to be upset with me." Let little Blake be upset! I would rather Blake be upset at you today than to be controlling you tomorrow. I recall a single mother who failed to be consistent in what I call "early correction for productive direction." Meaning, being consistent in confronting the negative behavior early on, then quickly correcting your child so he can separate from the thoughts and actions associated with the defiant behavior.

Back to the story about the single mom. By the time her son reached seventh grade he was ditching school and taking drugs. The counselor recommended the minor be enrolled into military school in order to instill structure and discipline in his life. The son had so much control over his mom to the point that she came to the office the next day to discharge herself and her son from counseling. The direction he was heading in life was definitely not a productive one.

What she saw early in her child should have been corrected while he was a child. Always remember these helpful nuggets. When it comes to correcting your child for the betterment of their social well-being, both present and future, your child's feelings take the backseat. Secondly, if your child cannot take instructions from you, then they most likely cannot take instructions from others.

I have specifically dedicated this chapter to giving you some helpful tips on how to be a wise overseer over your child's social conduct through vertical and horizontal relationships when in the discipline mode. You will grasp and eventually fall in love with this concept as you see the positive changes in your child's behavior and your ability to tell him what to do without repeating yourself over and over again. Note: If your child is beyond your control for correction, please seek counseling.

Vertical Relationship

It is all about the type of relationship you establish with your child that determines what you allow your child to do or not to do. There are essential elements that must be strategically in place before a healthy relationship can be in an operational mode. The four most important elements are love, respect, trust, and commitment, which I call the essential fours. These essential fours are a necessity to the health of your child's socio-emotional development.

Oftentimes when a child is about to face being disciplined by their parent or caregiver, their views on the situation are totally opposite from that of the parent. First of all, I have never heard of child who likes being corrected or disciplined for something they have done. If there is a child out there like that, they are few and far between.

Children may feel betrayed, hurt, and even unloved by their parents when being disciplined. We know this is not true; but in a child's mind their daddy or mommy "is being mean to me" or "they do not love me." That is why the love, trust, respect, and commitment, the essential four, must be set in place and recognized by both parties at their level of understanding. This way when the child is being disciplined, the essential four serve as a cushion that both the parent and child fall back on to console and mend the hurt little feelings and disappointments that have become the byproduct of disciplinary actions used to address an unacceptable behavior.

This cushion of love, trust, respect, and commitment also press out the tension after correction, which eventually reconnects both the parent and child, therefore strengthening the bond between the two. During this not-so-easy process of guiding your child in the right way, there is a maturation process occurring within the relationship taking it to another level.

Appropriate Time to Implement Vertical Relationship

There are two types of relationships you will engage in during the course of raising your child: vertical and horizontal. Vertical relationship is more firm, rigid, and instructional. Horizontal relationship is soft, nurturing, and validating. The key to being an effective overseer is knowing when it is appropriate to use either the vertical or horizontal relationship.

For example, you would not want to use the horizontal relationship when telling your child to sit down at home or in a public setting, especially when the child is not paying any attention to you. Why? "Sit down" is a command, not a request or plea. On the other hand, you definitely do not want to use the vertical relationship when you want to convey love or validation to your little one. This is a time of expressing how important your child is to you and how proud you are of him. You will notice over time that you will go from one relationship to another. You will also notice how both vertical and horizontal relationships complement each other. This brings a balance between loving your child and giving them tough, responsible love when needed.

Features of Vertical Relationship

There has to be some kind of way for you to determine when you are operating in a vertical relationship mode versus a horizontal mode, and there is. There are three notable features present to confirm when a parent and her child are functioning within a vertical relationship: voice distinction, expectancy of compliance, and parental consistency. Let's look at each feature independently to gain a better understanding of knowing when you and your child are actively participating in a vertical relationship.

Feature 1: Tone Distinctions

The tone of your voice will not only determine how effective you are when communicating to your child, but voice distinction will also determine how well your child responds to you based on the type of message you are trying to convey to her. Whether it be during a time of imparting wisdom, giving a command, making a request, being humorous, or even expressing your love towards your little one, there have to be what I call tone distinctions that properly carry the words spoken out of your mouth before the receiver responds accordingly.

There are four tone distinctions a parent should have in their arsenal: firm, loving, protective, and humorous. Tone distinctions are unique from the standpoint that they add a colorful variation to the words being projected out of your mouth so the receiver, your child, can audibly detect if the message being sent means Mom is serious or not. For example, when telling little Johnny to sit down, your tone might be firm and the message being sent is a command. Now little Johnny should automatically recognize and translate that this is your "I am not playing" tone and should be sitting down, like right now.

Voice distinctions can be a powerful communication tool, either verbally or nonverbally, but it is your responsibility to familiarize your child at an early age to the various tones you possess so they can effectively differentiate each tone and respond accordingly. You will find this will save you a lot of embarrassment, especially when you are out in public.

There is nothing worse than your child hearing you and doing the opposite of what you told them to do. I like what my husband said, "Even a dog knows how to distinguish the tone of your voice." Not to compare your child to a dog, but the point to be made is if a child is more intelligent than a dog, how much more should your child be able to distinguish the tone of your voice? It is all in what you allow your child to hear that will determine how they will respond.

The Begging Tone

When writing this section of the book, I thought I was finished. But my husband brought to my attention that I needed to briefly address to the parents the "no-no" tone, which is called the begging tone. You have heard of this tone before. As a matter of fact, you may have knowingly or unknowingly used this tone once or twice yourself. But there are parents out there who use this form of tone on a consistent basis.

This tone is a whiny plea a parent uses to get their child to obey. "Jason, come here!" "You guys stop right now and go to bed!" "Thomas, don't do that!" Really! When I overhear a parent begging their child to follow their instructions, it makes me cringe on the inside to the point that I want to tell the parent to step aside and let me speak on her behalf. I really want to say "Please hush!" but that would be rude.

Parents, the begging tone will only bring you frustration if you do not replace the begging tone with a more firm tone that will brings results. You may say, "I really have a high voice that sounds whiny." Well, you better go deep or make sure your high voice is firm; and do not make a habit of repeating yourself. A double whine is a no-no.

Believe it or not, a child can become so immune to a begging tone that she knows how to tune out her parents and ignore the instructions or commands being given to her. Why? This type of voice tone makes it seem optional for your child to obey or not obey. Keep in mind; obeying is not a choice, especially when the child is living under your roof. This is very unhealthy in a vertical relationship because not only is the child disrespecting your command or instruction, but she is also disrespecting your position as a parent. And parents, we did not have children to be disrespected. So practice your voice tone and say what you mean and mean what you say. Now I am finished!

Feature 2: Expectancy of Compliance

You will find that some children will try to test their parents to see how much they can really get away with before actually having to adhere to the commands or instructions that were given to them. They will wait until the last second to do what you told them to do five minutes ago.

One of my friends told me a story about her daughter being a tester as a young child. She and her husband had to constantly instruct their daughter, who at the time was three years old, to place her shoes neatly in a certain area of the kitchen before entering into the other areas of the house. This particular household custom was nothing new, but rather this structured routine had been around long enough for their daughter to be acclimated to her parents' expectations regarding this matter. However, the daughter would do just the opposite by putting her shoes in the family room, which was inches away from the designated area in the kitchen.

To top it off, the "little tester" did not follow the instructions of her parents right away, but she waited until the last second after her parents repeated themselves the second time. Well, you may say, "Sheryl, she finally did what her parents told her to do." No, she did not! And here's why: 1) The little girl did not place her shoes in the designated area she was told to place them in, the kitchen; and 2) She did not honor the instructions and commands of her parents in a timely manner but rather responded when she was ready.

The bottom line is, this little girl disobeyed her parents. Keep in mind; if your child half-way does what you told them to do, they are still being disobedient. However, the only exception to a child half-way doing what he or she is told to do without being disobedient is when a child is just learning or hearing the instructions or command being given to them for the first time. That is why it is important to model the instructions or commands for your child so they know how to respond accordingly.

I believe this leads perfectly into the second feature that makes up a vertical relationship, and that is expectancy of compliance. Expectancy of compliance refers to the time frame in which an instruction or command is expected to be acted upon. This is a very important feature because it has a two-fold purpose. First of all, this feature reinforces social skills such as listening and following instructions. Secondly, teaching your child to respect authority and compliance to rules becomes an essential element to the development of your child and the key to their success in life. Thirdly, this feature constantly makes the child cognizant of the importance of time and completing what needs to done within the time frame given. A side note to remember: The majority of a child's growing-up years is all about learning.

So the question still remains, how do I get my child to do what I ask him to do once I have released the command from my mouth?

1. Make sure the tone of your voice is firm, but not harsh.

2. Make sure the command or instruction being sent is clear, simple, and to the point. For example, if you want your child to clean up her room, I would recommend you show your child how you want her room to be cleaned so it meets your standards.

3. Make sure your standards are not too high for your child's age level or level of ability. Don't expect a four-year-old to change his bed linens or clean the mirror attached to his dresser.

4. Define the time frame in which you want the specific instruction or command to be carried out. It is important to realize that telling your child to cease from screaming in the grocery store should get an automatic response from you by giving your child the eye or telling him in a firm tone to stop.

On the other hand, there may be other instructions or commands that take a little longer for your child to respond to due to the complexity of the instruction or the steps it takes to fulfill the assignment accordingly. For instance, if you instruct your child to do her homework, remember that this particular command takes longer than sitting down and lowering her voice. And finally parents, be cognizant of your child's abilities and limitations and use that as a measuring tool to determine the time frame in which your child can comply effectively to the instructions or commands given to her.

If you noticed, I used the words "instruct" and "command" quite often in this chapter. Let me briefly separate the two in regards to their meaning because there is a distinctive difference between the two. When I refer to the word "instruction" (or instructions) I am basically referring to steps or orders in which you want things done. You might want your child to put away her toys, clean her room, and then take a bath. You are giving your daughter an order on how you want things done. By giving a command, I am referring to giving a direct order that demands an individual stops what he is doing and adhere. "Blake, stop pulling your sister's hair right now!" This is a command that demands an immediate response.

Feature 3: Parental Consistency:
Once, Maybe Twice, but Three Times, No!

How many times do you have to tell your child to do something or stop doing something before they do it? I often hear parents express their frustrations regarding the excessive amount of times they have to repeat themselves before their child finally listens and does what he was told. Parents who are constantly repeating themselves in hopes of being heard will remain frustrated until they learn how to do one thing: be consistent. Consistent in what? Consistent in keeping your word even if your child fails to adhere to what you say.

For example, you told London if she cleaned up her room she would be able to play with her dolls, but only after her room was clean. However, London decided she wanted to play with her dolls first and clean her room later. It is quite obvious London is not acknowledging your orders. Therefore she is being disrespectful to the one in charge, you. So what do you do? Do you let London continue playing with her dolls and clean up her room later? No! I hope this is not what you are doing in a real-life situation. The most effective way to handle this situation is by removing London's dolls and overseeing her while she cleans up her room.

Now, if you allow London to play with her dolls before she cleans up her room, not only will you miss out in giving London the opportunity to experience a teachable moment, but you will also be giving London leverage to prioritize what is important to her, therefore disregarding your orders.

Let me remind you again; we did not have children to be disrespected. Find some other activity London enjoys doing, but do not let her play with her dolls until she can respect you by following the instructions that were given to her. I bet if you try telling London to clean up her room tomorrow, she will do what she is told before she plays with her dolls. If not, do it again until she gets it.

Consistency means everything when you are parenting. Being consistent in executing the words coming out of your mouth is important simply because your child depends on you to be stable and reliable when no one else will. Never put yourself in what I call an "on" (consistent) and "off" (inconsistent) mode because you are setting yourself up for your child to give you an "on" (obedient) and "off" (disobedient) response. Your words are no good unless they are backed up by the actions supporting the words that were spoken. Finally, parental consistency is a treasure within itself because it teaches your child to honor and value the relationship that exists between the two of you.

Horizontal Relationship: The Balancer

I like to refer to this relationship as being the balancer. The horizontal relationship brings the balance between being firm, rigid, and instructional, which occurs during the vertical relationship, to becoming more soft, nurturing, and validating, which is received from the horizontal relationship. Each relationship carries within itself compartments where teachable moments can be pulled and used to help your child learn effective, instrumental, social, and emotional skills that can be used in relationships to come.

Vertical relationship is constantly in operation mode, just like a diner that stays open 24/7. There is a constant adult/child, mentor/mentee, or teacher/student interaction taking place while instructing the child what to do and not to do. In other words, firmness, instructions, and rigidity are constant factors implemented during the course of raising your child, but they should not solely be the only form of relationship you and your child operate within.

Your child is not drafted into a military camp, but rather birthed into a family system were order and structure are provided so they can grow and develop into a responsible and productive adult. The balance received from the horizontal relationship steps into added moments of softness, encouragement, validation, and love. These are all the byproducts of nurturing, which is purposefully designed to care for the growth and development of your child. The horizontal relationship has the ability to do the following:

1. Reduce the tension between parent and child after correctional or disciplinary measures.

2. Reaffirm the child's value to the family.

3. Acknowledge the child's accomplishments.

4. Encourage the child that they can.

5. Love your child unconditionally and reassure them you will always be there.

Different forms of interaction are taking place during each relationship, and each relationship is better equipped to address a certain situation that occurs during parent/child interaction. These interactions still run parallel to each other, taking turns to either implement structure (vertical relationship) or balancing everything out with love, affection, and encouragement. Both vertical and horizontal relationships can serve as a powerful team when used at the appropriate time.

When to and How to

The softness, encouragement, validation, love, and affection constituting a horizontal relationship should never be used sparingly or implemented when it is absolutely necessary. There should be a constant outpouring of parental love and affection that not only solidifies the existence of our children, but also gives our children the opportunity to learn through modeling that caring for and loving someone is part of life. The uniqueness of the horizontal relationship is that it allows you the opportunity to participate in shaping your child's intrapersonal and interpersonal skills. Most importantly, a horizontal relationship teaches your child how to embrace healthy relationships while the vertical relationship teaches your child how to honor relationships.

Tough Love and Protective Love

I would like to conclude this chapter by briefly discussing the two types of love: tough love and protective love. Both of these operate within the domain of the horizontal relationship. Each type of love is a must-have when raising your child for the simple fact that one is used more often than the other during different stages of your child's life. For example, protective love is highly activated during their infant and adolescent years and tough love more so during their teenage and young-adult years. Both types of love can be used anytime during the course of raising you child based on the situation at hand. Tough love is what I call "letting them find out for themselves that what they wanted in life was not all it added up to be." Tough love is most commonly used when your child rejects your guidance by doing just the opposite of what you advised him to do. Protective love is the combination of both the nurturing and overseer role of a parent constantly looking out for the safety of their child.

Reflections

Reflections

PUBLIC SOCIAL GRACE

The only way your child can understand how to properly conduct herself in a public setting is by you taking quality time to teach her. But how can one expect a child to act appropriately in public if you, the parent, lack public social grace? If you have not figured it out by now, this chapter will focus on the following:

1) Defining public social grace.
2) The importance of teaching your child social etiquettes.
3) The different forms of public etiquettes.
4) Strategies to effectively teach public social grace.

I always like to share a story or give illustrations to support the concepts being presented in this book, so here I go. My husband and I travel extensively with our company, either by plane or car. One hot summer day, Shawn and I were traveling to North Carolina by car. We needed to stop to refuel and also use the restroom. While

Shawn was pumping gas in our SUV, I went inside the convenience store to use the restroom. As I proceeded back to the front entrance of the convenience store, I noticed a mother and her daughter, no more than three or four feet away, heading towards me.

I greeted both the mother and her daughter with a pleasantly warm smile while I held the door for them to enter in. Wouldn't you know, the mother walked via the door while holding her daughter's hand and not once did she say thank you or did she smile. As a matter of fact, she did not even acknowledge my presence. It was as if the doors opened automatically and she and her daughter just walked in. Wow!

It was quite evident this mother was modeling a behavior she thought was appropriate enough for her daughter to emulate. How sad! There was an open window available for this mother to seize the moment and model before her child how to conduct herself properly in a public setting. Instead this mother chose to miss this priceless opportunity. If this mother continues exposing her daughter to this cold, dysfunctional behavior, her daughter will eventually become a spitting image of her mother.

I had a recent experience at Ross that was just the opposite of this story. It was a beautiful Sunday afternoon in Georgia. I decided to go to Ross after church to do some light shopping. As I was casually looking through the dress rack, there were two little girls playing with a shopping cart a few feet away from me. As I was approaching the end of the dress rack, the two little girls lost control of the shopping cart and the cart was heading towards my black stylish leather pumps. Their eyes and mouth were wide open as I stopped the cart from running over my feet. I gently patted one of the little girls that was closest to me and told her to be careful. Their mother immediately responded by having her daughters apologize to me.

With beautiful smiles on their faces, the little girls obeyed their mother's orders. In both instances the mothers were given the window of opportunity to do right by their daughters by exposing to their eye and ear gate the appropriate social skills to use while conducting themselves out in public. The difference between the two is one mother chose not to, while the other one did. One mother was considerate of others and the other could have cared less.

There was a profound message I saw on a billboard sitting high on top of a building in St. Louis that I believe sums up both incidences: "They (children) become who you (parent) are. In other words, your children are a reflection of you—either good or bad.

Importance of Social Grace

You will find if you do not place a value on a thing, it will eventually become insignificant; and anything that is insignificant becomes obsolete. Things that are of value or of importance are constantly being used because they serve a purpose (i.e., emotional, physical, social, spiritual, etc.) in the lives of those who take advantage of what they have to offer. However, an individual will never get the most of something if they do not place a high value on its existence.

For example, we as humans place a high value on food because we understand the vital role it plays in providing the necessary nutrients for energy utilized during daily physical activities. The high value our society places on food should be even greater when it comes to the social development of our children if we expect to reap the benefits in the long run. What benefits? 1) your child not being an embarrassment, but a positive representation of you when out in public; and 2) your child excelling in school and in life because he is socially graced to interact with others and conduct himself in such a manner that doors of opportunity are constantly opening for him.

However, if you do not see any value in your child's social development and you allow your child to act any kind of way, there will definitely be no positive benefits for you to reap. Instead you will be confronted with frustration, hurt, disappointment, and embarrassment, which all stem from a child that is socially undeveloped. You have to see your family and child as a business. If you own your own business or if you are employed by a company, you are well aware of the fact that a business or organization is only as successful or productive as the employees representing the company or organization.

There are companies out there that have either failed or have been rated poorly because of 1) the inconsistency on behalf of the employees in providing quality customer service; 2) the lack of commitment, unprofessionalism; and 3) being unethical and immoral. The list can go on and on.

My point is this. It is the responsibility of the CEO of the company or the managerial staff of the organization to hire people who have similar values and work ethics represented by the company. By doing so the organization's cultural makeup (characteristics, values, behaviors, etc.) will remain intact in order for the goals of the company to be successfully met (Daft, 2011). The leader of the organization takes responsibility in hiring the right people because they value the existence of the organization and what the organization has to offer to its consumers.

The same applies to you. Your child represents you, and what you deposit in him socially is what others will visibly see when he is at school, church, at the mall, etc. In other words, your child is a reflection of you. When your child is away from your presence, people should see you in your child. Just like if I never get the opportunity to meet the owner of the company, the employees should be a reflection of the owner. Got it?

So now this changes things. You are not just raising a child for the sake of raising a child. You are overseeing a family system or "family business" that requires everyone who is part of this system to be appropriately aligned with the existing cultural makeup of the family system.

The Origin of Public Social Grace

Any and everything, good or bad, that exists on this earth has a starting point or origin—even your child's social development.

Now, Now! I know I have been using social skills, behavior, and public social grace (or etiquettes) interchangeably, but actually they are different. Social skills are an accumulation of techniques, such as saying "Excuse me," "No thank you," or a friendly smile an individual acquires by learning and is released through one's behavioral expressions.

Behaviors are the physical manifestation of one's social skills. Behavioral expressions are either in compliance or not in compliance with the standard public etiquettes that are an integral part of societal norm. Public social grace is an individual's ability of knowing how to carry himself before he actually goes out in public; in other words, knowing what to do before doing it. Public social grace is also an individual's ability to carry himself in such a pleasing manner that it attracts favorable attention or admiration from those he comes in contact with. I like to say there is a natural flow in how an individual conducts himself when out in public.

As I indicated earlier, any and everything, either good or bad, has a starting point, including the behavior of your child. I also indicated that one's behavior is an expression or physical manifestation of the social skills that are acquired through learning. I want to focus specifically on this word "learn" from the standpoint that what you have learned throughout the course of life has an origin. This can be through what you have heard or seen on a continual basis, or repetitious information that is processed in the mind, which is commonly referred to as the thought process.

This thought process consists of the conscious, subconscious, and conscience. The conscious level of the mind intercepts the information that is presented or released, either physically or verbally, by concentrating on what is being said or done in an effort to gain understanding. This information is then passed on to subconscious. The subconscious level of the thought process has three functions:

1. It records or memorizes the information introduced to your mind.

2. It transports the information to the third level of thought process, which is called the conscience or the belief system.

3. It retrieves the information stored in the conscience and serves as an autopilot which assists you in responding to familiar situations and performs a certain task while doing something else at the same time (i.e., driving a car and talking on the cell phone at the same time).

The conscience level of the mind is what I call the acceptance and rejection center. The values, beliefs, social skills, opinions, intellectual information, and routines that already reside in your conscience or belief system are constantly being used as a reference point to compare newly received information to determine if it lines up with existing information. It can replace the existing information or be denied entrance altogether into your belief system.

So let me give you a practical illustration of how your thought process works. Can you remember the first time your learned how to drive? Most likely when you stepped into the car and got behind the wheel you did not want the radio on and you did not want anyone to say a word to you, especially if the conversation was not pertaining to driving. You did not even want to hear a bird chirp. You wanted everything and everyone to be in silent mode so you could concentrate on the driving instructions you received from the person who was bold enough to get in the car with you and teach you how to drive.

All the information received while driving (i.e., turn your signal lights on before making a left turn, etc.) was intercepted by the conscious level of your thought process and then passed on to your subconscious, which started to record the driving instructions. The subconscious transported the driving instructions to your conscience where the information was placed on file for future reference.

Now when you drive, you can simultaneously talk on the phone, put your makeup on (ladies), comb your hair, or listen to music because your subconscious has gone to the conscience and retrieved the information associated with driving. It begins to set itself on autopilot so you can drive effortlessly and concentrate on other things.

Now you have a better understanding of why it is crucial for you to be cognizant of what you say or do in the presence of your child. It is your responsibility to expose your child's ear gate and eye gate, the paths that lead to her mind, to words and actions that will not only shape her belief system in a positive and productive way, but also keep you from experiencing embarrassment.

A former business client of mine told me the story of going to a high-end restaurant in Rhode Island to have lunch with her sister. A short distance from her table was a man and his four-year-old daughter, also having lunch. The girl pointed over to the table where my former client and her sister were sitting and said out loud, "Daddy, is that what a "N" looks like?" The father scolded his daughter and told her to be quite. Mrs. B. just smiled and looked at the father, who held his head down in shame. This little girl was only repeating what she heard (the ear gate exposure) over and over again at home. What you expose your child to at home, good or bad, will eventually come out in the open. Just make sure what comes out of your child's mouth is what you want others to hear.

Let me briefly provide you with one more piece of vital information I know will be helpful to you. Did you know that what you allow your child to get away with, such as temper tantrums or falling out when he does not get his way or hitting you in the face when he is angry at you, can take root into his belief system if you do not correct his inappropriate behavior at the onset? I call inappropriate behaviors that are unaddressed at the onset but are rather passively attended to, if at all, slip-bys."

For example, your darling little Joe hit you on your leg because you told him he could not have a certain toy. Instead of grabbing darling little Joe's hand, looking him straight in his eyes, and telling him with a serious look on your face that it is not nice to hit Mommy and do not do that again (vertical relationship), you let him keep hitting you while periodically telling him to stop as you continue shopping in the store. WRONG! You just sent a message to your child that it is OK to be disrespectful towards you. As a result, this nonreactive, distorted information has slipped by and entered into his thought process. It will eventually become part of his belief system, where he receives instruction on how to respond to situations.

I was sitting in my car in the parking lot of the Dollar Tree store, enjoying the cool breeze and a moment of silence, when all of a sudden I heard someone screaming. The carrier of this disruptive noise was drawing closer towards me, and to my surprise it was a little girl, about six or seven, screaming and hitting her mother while walking towards their car.

The daughter was extremely mad at her mother from whatever took place prior to my being exposed to this dramatic episode. Since my moment of serenity was disrupted, I thought I should at least stick around to see how this would play out. The mother never looked down at her daughter, but rather kept looking straight ahead while proceeding to her car. They both got in the car, and all of a sudden the mother said a couple of words to her daughter.

What did she do that for? Whatever the mother said to her daughter made things even worse. The little girl came from the backseat of the car to the front seat and got in her mother's face to voice her anger even more. Wow! I can assure you this was not the first time this gentle little princess had ever been disrespectful towards her mother. This definitely was a learned behavior.

She most likely witnessed another adult figure in her household disrespecting her mother in the same fashion and watched her mom respond in a nonreactive manner. This little girl's belief system was molded by what she had seen and heard in her home environment, therefore dictating how she should respond to situations that caused her to become angry. Food for thought: What you allow to slip by and enter into the mind of your child will eventually become your reality, good or bad.

The Must Haves

There are so many dos and don'ts when it comes to public social graces, also referred to as social etiquettes, that it would take a whole book in itself to properly address this subject. However, I want to briefly address what I consider the bare essentials of social skills your child needs to have when out in public. I called these bare essentials the "Must Haves of Social Grace" simply because they:

1. establish a framework in which other social skills can be built upon;
2. help the child to understand and respect boundaries outside of their home environment;
3. strengthen the child's interpersonal skills;
4. constantly challenges the child to go beyond self in order to understand the world around him; and they
5. allow him to not only witness but also experience the positive reactions given for displaying positive social skills.

Must Have #1: Respecting Others' Personal Space

This Must Have does not happen automatically. Just like the majority of the Must Haves there are opportunities in which the parent is able to address and correct their child's behavior while in action. A child does not fully understand she is invading someone's personal space unless she is made aware and corrected in the midst of the act.

You may wonder, *Why do I need to correct my child right, on the spot?* So that your child can make the right connection between his behavior and the appropriate behavior that should have been used when violating someone's personal space (i.e., the child not paying attention where he is going and runs into someone, etc.)

Bless his little heart; it's not that the child is intentionally trying to violate someone's personal space. Because he is so carefree and playful he is constantly in the learning mode. He needs to be led and guided so he can properly maneuver himself accordingly when out in public. Boundaries are meaningless to a child, so someone's personal space is definitely not of importance. Therefore, the following plan needs to be in place when you take your child out into a public setting:

1. Go over the rules and expectations you have of your child when she is in the presence of others. For example, "Keep your hands to yourself" or "No running in the store."

2. Survey your surroundings before you and your child venture out. A quick survey enables you to determine what your child can or cannot do. For instance, if you and your child are going to the store, then your child should not be running up and down the aisles. She should be walking close to you, and younger children should be sitting in the basket.

3. Monitor the whereabouts of your child at all times. Make sure he is not in an area he is not supposed to be in or doing something he should not be doing. In most cases a child violates an individual's space because the child is somewhere he should not be.

4. Have your child apologize (if she is old enough to speak) or apologize yourself on behalf of your child. By having your child apologize or apologizing on behalf of your child you are letting the person know your child is still a work in progress. You are also acknowledging and respecting that person's space.

I was attending a dinner event and before dinner was actually served, people were mingling and getting aquatinted with each other. I happened to find a quiet, cozy little section in the room where I could be observant, like I normally do. However, my cozy, quiet place was quickly interrupted and occupied by two ladies. As I briefly engaged in conversation with both of the ladies, a little girl about three years old came along, putting her hands all over my white pants and stepping all over me in order to get to her mother, who was sitting on the sofa next to mine.

Rather than stopping her daughter in her tracks and encouraging her to say "Excuse me," the mother allowed her daughter to proceed until she reached her destination. I don't blame the child, but I do blame the mother for the simple fact that she allowed her daughter to violate my personal space without addressing and correcting her in the midst of the act. What the mother should have done was instruct her child to say "Excuse me" or apologize on behalf of her child. By doing so the little girl could have made a connection between the inappropriate behavior and the more suitable behavior for the situation at hand.

Now I was put in a dilemma of letting the child continue invading my personal space or correcting the child and taking a chance that the mother would not get offended. Granted, the mother may not have thought there was anything wrong with this act because her daughter was "just a child." However, this does not erase the fact that this mother was responsible for her child's actions. Training her child to be socially appropriate is an ongoing process. Now this child has to wait for a teacher or another adult figure to educate her on this misinterpreted social grace. Before you can effectively teach your child to respect the personal space of others, you first must see the value of doing so yourself.

Must Have #2: "Say "Excuse Me" When I Am Talking to an Adult

How many times have you witnessed a child interrupting their parents while they were conversing with another adult? The child either kept patting their parents on the arm or leg; started talking over the existing conversation, yelling "Mom or Dad" as if they were miles away; or had a tantrum. A child feels what he has to say is of the utmost importance for that moment and everything else can wait.

This may sound rude, but there is a logical reason behind this selfish behavior. We as humans automatically come out of our mother's womb in what I call the self-centered or I need mode: "I need my diaper changed!" "I need to be fed!" or "I need to be held!" The list can go on and on. This egocentric mind-set a child possesses is an adaptive process used during infancy and is quite effective as it serves to ensure the infant's needs are met.

The infant is totally dependent on her parents to meet her basic needs (i.e., food, shelter, love, etc.) in order to live. As the child gets older she is still depending on her parents to meet her needs, but not at the degree she was during the infancy stage of development. However, when a child is not properly weaned off this self-centered or "I" mode, this egocentric mind-set is visibly seen through the behavior and conversation of a child, therefore she is labeled maladaptive and rude.

For the most part, your child's needs or wants are validated and require your attention. But there has to be a pivotal moment in your child's life where the level of respect in which they make their requests known is a sign of social maturity. This sign (social maturity) becomes a reality only by you, the parent, by guiding and instructing your child to look beyond self.

This "Must Have" is essential from the standpoint that you are given the opportunity to teach your child how to be a giver and not always a receiver. A child that says "Excuse me" in order to get the attention of his parent while his parent is talking to another adult is indirectly conveying a message to his parent. He acknowledges the fact his parent is in the middle of a conversation and wants to give them the respect they deserve by saying "Excuse me." That is public social grace at its best. So how do you activate this Must Have?

1. Start at Home. One of the best educational institutional settings in the world is one's home environment. Granted, in order for the home environment to be qualified as one of the top educational institutions existing in our society, parents must be socially and emotionally sound. They must constantly display this from of soundness in the presence of their children.

Practice this Must Have (Say "Excuse Me" When I Am Talking to an Adult) at home through role-playing different scenarios where your child has to say "Excuse me" before being acknowledged. Role-playing is a fun activity for a child because children love to pretend or make believe. In the midst of this enjoyable event, make sure your child is getting the most out of understanding the importance of saying "Excuse me." Also how being acknowledged by you will be an automatic response when she respects you when you are conversing with another adult.

2. Reverse Roles. This is another form of role-playing, but this time you allow the child to pretend he is the adult. This role reversal activity allows your child to experience what an adult or parent feels when they are rudely interrupted while talking to another adult. It also causes the child to understand the importance of hearing the words "Excuse me" and the association it has to be acknowledged by another individual. The purpose of this technique is to challenge the child to differentiate between being rude and being considerate or respectful.

3. Do Not Acknowledge. This can be one of the most challenging steps when it comes to training your child how to say "Excuse me" when two adults are talking. Why? You are tempted to acknowledge the child without correcting her for the sake of not being embarrassed. Parents, you are going to have to toughen up and accept being respected as an adult. If your child fails or refuses to say "Excuse me," just ignore her. Someone may say ignoring the child is being rude. No, that is not being rude. That is refusing to tolerate a behavior that can have a stagnating effect on her social development. If she continues, politely excuse yourself from the adult you are conversing with and firmly tell your child to say "Excuse me" if she wants to be acknowledged.

Some kids can be very stubborn and sometimes resistant, but stand your ground; mean what you say and say what you mean. The person who does not give in wins. Just keep talking to the other adult and she will process what is going on and make the adjustments accordingly. When you are at home or in the car, just go over this Must Have and ask your child the following question to refresh her memory: "When I am talking to another adult and you want Mommy's attention, what must you say?" and wait for her answer. Remember, what your child gets away with is based on what you allow her to get away with.

4. Recognize and Compliment. When your child successfully adheres to this Must Have, either at home or in public, give him a compliment. Compliments encourage your child to repeat the appropriate social behavior you desire and he needs during his social development.

Must Have #3: "Talk to Me Correctly"

What tone of voice does your child exert when they speak to you while in private or public? Are you comfortable with your child saying "What?" or "Yeah!" in response to your giving them instructions, asking a question, or trying to get their attention? Are you OK with your child speaking to you as if you were their equal rather than their elder or parent? Would you consider it a big deal if your child yelled at you in front of others because they could not get their way?

These questions definitely are not far-fetched but rather a reality in today's society. Nowadays parents are so overly consumed with fulfilling the demands of life that they are not sensitive to what they need to hear. In other words, their timing is off when it comes to actually listening to and correcting the child as needed while dialoguing.

Oftentimes what occurs in the midst of being occupied with life and constantly on the go is that a child may say something disrespectful. As a result, you may respond in one or all of the following ways: 1) you don't say anything at all; 2) you roll your eyes in frustration; 3) you give your child the evil look; or 4) you tell your child to shut up, which is just a bad as the child talking to you disrespectfully.

The parent never really addresses the child's inappropriate remarks, and as a result, the inappropriate remarks become a template the child uses to respond to their parents at home or in public. You would be totally surprised at some of the things children say to their parents:

"You can't tell me what to do!" "Shut up!" "Leave me alone!" "I'm going to tell Daddy on you!" "I hate you!"

I don't know why parents, not all, get so weak when it comes to disciplining their children. It is as if they cannot stand for their child to be upset or mad at them. Please! There will always be a time in everyone's life when a child will be upset or angry, and your child is definitely not exempt. The good thing is, children do not stay angry for very long. It may take a moment for them to process whatever they are upset about, but they will eventually get over it like nothing ever happened.

I guess the bottom line to all this disrespectful madness is, the level of respect a parent establishes for themselves will determine how they will allow people to talk to them, especially their child. I am warning you; if you permit your child to talk any way at home, he will do the same when you are in public. You cannot cover up respect or disrespect for the simple fact it has its own way of surfacing to the top.

Why is this Must Have a must when it comes to public social grace? For the simple reason you are teaching your child how to be respectful towards their elder through words. This becomes a vital social skill from the standpoint that your child should be able to effectively communicate with others outside of their home environment. Can I let you in on a little secret? People really do not want to be bothered with rude and inconsiderate children. This might be the answer to someone's question out there regarding why it is do difficult to find a babysitter for your child.

Appropriate Steps to Activate This "Must Have"

1. Be cognizant of what you say and how you say it when speaking to another adult in the presence of your child or when speaking directly to another child. If you are always responding to your spouse by saying "What?" don't be surprised when your child responds to you by saying "What?" Words that

take root and become common phrases or replies in one's household set the language standard of how your child will converse when out in public.

2. Constantly implement or interject pleasant words throughout the day, in different settings, where your child's ear gate is consistently being exposed to language that is suitable. This daily process will help program your child's thoughts with words that will assist him in thinking right, believing right, behaving right, and speaking right.

3. Correct your child when she speaks out of line with you or another adult. I call this step "on-the-spot correction," which is better known as nipping it in the bud. On-the-spot correction is quite effective because the child is being corrected right in the midst of the inappropriate action.

Redirecting your child's words and addressing the attitude associated with the inappropriate words create a teachable moment (the open window) that mentally influences your child to make a connection between speaking respectfully versus speaking disrespectfully. If your child's unruly remarks towards you or another adult are not corrected on the spot, this validates the child's behavior and indirectly coveys to the child that she is free to speak to others as she pleases.

Must Have #4: Excuse Me and Thank You

This Must Have is so similar to Must Have #3 because it does require a child to use their words in the proper context when participating in public conversation. This Must Have of public social grace also teaches a child the importance of being grateful, appreciative, and considerate during social interactions. A child that is grateful, appreciative, and considerate socially is what I call being pleasingly polite. A pleasingly polite child has been taught to not take for granted that someone has to do anything for him, but rather that individual does it out of the kindness of their heart. A pleasingly polite child is not only grateful or appropriate, but finds a sense of joy or accomplishment when given the opportunity to be considerate toward others.

For example, a little boy opens the door for a woman as she enters the store. This Must Have, saying "Excuse me" and "Thank you," births favor into your child's life for years to come because people are willing to give of their time, wisdom, and influence to a person that is sincerely grateful and considerate of others. A child that always feels entitled, never grateful, and never seizes the moment of being considerate towards others will most likely grow up to not only be disrespectful towards others, but also one who manipulates his social environment.

The best way to effectively cultivate this social skill into your child's life is by actively demonstrating this Must Have both at home and in public. Set up "Thank you" and "Excuse me" moments at home that allow your child to both observe and do. For example, at the dinner table ask your child to please pass you the bread or whatever food item that is easy for him to handle, and respond by saying, "Thank you." There is so much your child can learn from you; you just have to be willing to teach him. Remember, your family is your business, so invest in your business wisely.

Must Have # 5: Be Calm When You Don't Get Your Way

At the airport in Dallas, my husband and I were patiently waiting to board our connecting flight to Atlanta. I noticed a two-year-old boy stretched out on the floor and having a tantrum while his parents were helplessly standing there. Every time the father made an attempt to pick up his son so he and his wife could proceed to their designated gate, the little boy would resist by crying a little louder. I thought this was a downright shame for a little boy to have that much control over his parents to the point that his behavior was becoming socially embarrassing.

I can recall another incident where my husband and I were doing a children's concert at a local elementary school in West Memphis, Arkansas. There was a long line filled with parents and children who were eagerly waiting to purchase the musical products being sold after the concert. Next in line to be served was a beautiful couple and their two boys, ages six and eight.

The parents were trying to decide what CDs to buy that would be age appropriate for both of their children. However, the younger of the two brothers had another plan. He wanted the CD that had all of the songs performed during the concert, while his parents were leaning more towards purchasing a CD that would be suitable for both of their children.

After it was all said and done, the little boy did not get what he wanted. Nevertheless, he did not cry; nor did he fall on the floor and have a tantrum. Instead he quietly walked away disappointed, yet still kept his composure. I said to myself, *Wow! This little boy learned a vital social skill that allowed him to conduct himself accordingly while in public.*

Any time a child can keep his composure in the midst of not getting his way is exemplifying public social grace at its best. Why? He had learned to not let his emotions dictate to him when things do not necessarily go his way. Don't get me wrong; he may not like the fact that he did not get the CD he wanted. He may even have shed some tears when he got home. But his emotions were not controlling his behavior to the point that he was socially disruptive.

Can you imagine a child just the opposite of what I described who did not get what he wanted? He probably would fall on the floor kicking and screaming, or jump up and down, shouting at the top of his lungs. This type of behavior is definitely considered as being socially disruptive, which is a byproduct of a child's unwillingness to control his emotions when things are not going his way. His method of operation, having a tantrum, is put into operation when he is being denied what he desires to have; when the "I" mode of operation is being challenged. Just think; if this child is never corrected, he will carry this socially disruptive behavior into adulthood. An adult that is social disruptive through tantrums is like an oversized baby needing a bottle to calm him down.

Being socially disruptive by way of displaying temper tantrums in public is a power-control move to bring embarrassment or guilt to the other person, usually the parent, who can provide the child what she wants. Tantrums are not activated by a need, but rather a want. Have you ever heard of a child having a temper tantrum because she wanted a bath? Hmm! Tantrums are basically put into action when a "want" is not being met at the time the recipient, the child, and some adults, think it should be met, which is usually right now, this very second.

Before I give you the steps needed to effectively train your child how to display self-composure when in public, I want to go back to the two-year-old at the airport in Dallas. This little boy was definitely being validated by his action because his parents were not doing their part in nipping this socially unacceptable behavior in the bud. I can assure you this is not the first time this child displayed this type of behavior in public. Either the parents did not know what to do or they thought he would just grow out of it.

What the parents should have done was pick up the child in the midst of the tantrum and proceed to their gate so they could catch their flight on time. Secondly, they should have modified their voice tone to a more firm, I-mean-business type of tone, as an indicator that he needed to wrap up his drama act and behave accordingly.

Finally, his parents must be consistently diligent in not giving into their child's tantrums. By consistently addressing his tantrum each time he has one, it will eventually register in the child's thought processes that his method of operation is being weakened by his parents' not giving in to his unacceptable behavior, but rather putting a stop to it.

For example, Alex begins to softly cry in the toy store because you did not purchase the doll she wanted. You on the other hand recognize that Alex's softly crying is your forewarning sign that Alex is about to break out into a tantrum because you did not get her what she wanted at the time she wanted it. Her egocentric mentality is dominating her emotions and her emotions are dominating her behavior.

Keep your composure and gently lean over and look Alex directly in the eye and firmly say, "Find your quiet voice right now." Her eyes should get big for the simple fact you have caught on to her method of operation as it relates to having a tantrum. Parents who are dealing with a child who has tantrums must recognize the forewarning signs and then immediately address them. You will save yourself a lot of time, energy, and embarrassment.

How to Decrease Temper Tantrums and Increase Self-composure

1. Be Patient. This negative behavior did not develop overnight, so it will not disappear overnight. Temper tantrums come into existence by one or all of the following ways:

1. The child was not properly weaned off the egocentric mentality.
2. The parent failed to correct the child the first time he displayed a tantrum in public and at home.
3. The child is emulating what he observed on television, at school, in the presence of his cousins, or other public settings that can have a negative influence on his behavior.

By practicing patience you are acknowledging that your child's thought process needs to be reprogrammed in order to undo and replace this inappropriate behavior associated with not getting his way.

2. Recognize the Forewarning Signs of a Tantrum. A child known for having tantrums normally has what I call "forewarning" signs that lead up to the actual temper tantrum. Forewarning signs are different for each child. A child may start off crying softly then gradually escalate as time progresses before actually displaying a full-blown tantrum. Another child may start off whining, rubbing her head, or twisting her hair around her finger while pleading for what she wants. If the whining, rubbing, twisting, and pleading does not work, you have given the child no other choice but to have a full-blown tantrum.

Sometimes there are no forewarning signs at all. The child will just fall on the floor and start kicking and screaming. You, the parent, should know your child better than anyone else. Recognizing and immediately addressing the forewarning signs are to your advantage from the standpoint that you can command him to stop what he is doing at that moment.

3. Overlook the Embarrassment. I sometimes think this is the most difficult thing for a parent to do: overlooking the embarrassment of your child being out of control and people wondering what you are going to do. I say get over the embarrassment, because being embarrassed will make you do things you should not be doing just for the sake of not being embarrassed.

Oh, you see it all the time, a parent giving a child a cookie or special treat or what they actually want to keep them quiet; or a parent leaving a special event simply because their child is being disruptive. Wrong! A parent should never give into a tantrum, but rather confront the tantrum head-on, especially if you missed or responded too late to the forewarning signs. It's like the child has an inner knowledge that if he acts up, Mom and Dad will give him what he wants because they do not want to be embarrassed.

When it comes to feeling embarrassed, look at it from this perspective. The only cause of embarrassment is not your child having a tantrum in public. It is also because your parental skills are being showcased in front of strangers who are waiting to see what you are going to do. My advice to you is, don't be moved by what other people think; especially people you do not even know and probably will never see again. Focus on correcting your child and move on.

4. Do Not Reward the Behavior. When your child has a tantrum, do not reward the negative behavior. Why? By rewarding a negative behavior instead of correcting it you are condoning the act. For example, Matthew just had a tantrum in the mall. After you finally resolve the matter, or when Matthew finally gets tired of being on the floor and decides the performance is over, you treat him to some ice cream. What is wrong with this picture?

You are rewarding the behavior. In other words, the socially disruptive behavior, the tantrum, is too closely associated with receiving a treat: delicious ice cream. Another example. Jessica had a tantrum in the store the day before and you go back to the store to purchase the doll she wanted. Really! You are rewarding or validating the negative behavior.

A parent who is guilty of doing either one of the examples I just provided is: 1) allowing their child to hold on to her egocentric mentality; 2) denying the child the opportunity to make the connection that this type of behavior is unacceptable and will not influence the parent in giving in to what the child wants; 3) promoting the negative behavior; and 4) failing to teach their child self-composure.

5. Acknowledge the Positive Behavior. You do not always have to purchase a toy or take your child out for a special treat when he refrains from having a tantrum. You will find your child is just as happy to be praised with words (i.e., "I am so proud of you for controlling your emotions today!"). You do not have to buy your child something every time he does something he should have been doing all along. However, if you insist in buying little Johnny something special, take him back to the store where he had the tantrum and buy him the truck he wanted but did not get the first time because of his award-winning performance the week before. Remind him the reason why he is receiving the truck is because you are extremely proud of him for not crying and falling on the floor (verbally describe the signs to him so he knows that you know his method of operation).

Must Have #6: Greetings

I realize some kids are more social than others, but that is no excuse for you not to teach your child how to greet others in public. It is so unwise to limit your child's human contact to just you, those in your household, and maybe some close relatives. There is a world out there waiting for your child to practice his language and interpersonal skills.

I am definitely not saying to rush your child to become social due to the fact that the development of children's social skills is not the same. It develops at their level of comfort or what they have been exposed to at home through parental interaction. However, what I am saying is you can practice with your child at home in order to develop this simple and polite social skill of greeting someone. Practice saying "Good morning" when she gets up in the morning. I recommend you say this phrase even before she starts talking. Why? You are imparting positive repetitious information into her thought process. This is being stored and made readily available when the right time presents itself.

A simple technique such as role-playing with your child on how to greet others with a smile, how to greet someone by saying hello, or responding to someone by greeting them, can make a world of a difference. What you teach your child is what she will do. Keep in mind; if you are not a social person, don't expect your child to be sociable. Work on your social skills first; then teach your child. To greet someone has never hurt anyone, but rather brought a smile to that individual's face.

Reflections

Reflections

by speaking, hearing, and seeing words or images that support the existence of the selected images dominating your child's thoughts. You may desire your child to do well in school, so the preselected words or phrases you may have chosen such as "You are smart" and the preselected image you may have chosen is surrounding your child around other children that are academically inclined.

I can truly say that my sister-in-law has this reprogramming process, along with the other two active elements of purposeful thinking, down pat. She is constantly challenging her daughter, my niece, to reprogram her mind by surrounding her with friends and educationally based material that reflects the image branded in my niece's mind. By strengthening her academic skills outside of the school environment, and by her parents validating her through words, my niece is identified as being intelligent. As a result, her thoughts are reflected through her behavior in regards to her studies, loving to learn, high academic performance, and the ability to speak two languages. Her parents gave her what they wanted her to consider and now she is responding accordingly. Wow!

Not all thoughts should be passed down to your child, especially if those thoughts contradict living a productive, healthy, honest, and peaceful life. Remember, I referred to the statement I saw on a billboard in St. Louis that said, "They become who you are." Well, your child also becomes who they are based on the thoughts you verbally express to them on a frequent basis. Your thoughts, either good or bad, take root in your child's thought process and begin to dictate to her emotions. They then eventually manifest through her behavior. I call this process the "transference of thoughts."

Parental thoughts that are verbally or physically expressed are actually being transferred into the child's thought process through words and images. The mind is so powerful that someone can say a word like "dog" and automatically the image of a dog will pop in your mind. The mind is like an artist; it can draw a picture on the canvas of your imagination in a matter of seconds just by words spoken.

So the questions you need to ask yourself and honestly answer are,

"What thoughts are having a negative impact on my life?" And, "Am I willing to change my negative thoughts and adopt positive thoughts that will assure my words and behavior will shape and influence my child's thoughts in a positive as opposed to a negative way?"

Think about a parent who is always depressed and sad and only speaks doom and gloom in the presence of their child. It is not that this parent is intentionally doing this, but a specific mind-set was dominating the parent's thoughts and emotions before the child was ever born. As a result, the negativity that has plagued this parent's communication style, thoughts, emotions, and behavioral patterns has transferred or spilled over into the thoughts, emotions, actions, and verbal expressions of their child. In other words, the child has inherited the mind-set of their parent.

Sadly, there are a lot of selfish parents out there who are unwilling to replace their negative, nonproductive thoughts for more healthy, positive, and productive thoughts that will nourish and produce a purposeful thinking pattern; especially when it has been brought to the parents' attention that their way of thinking is not beneficial to them or their child. Willingness to change is the key to progress.

Here are some simple steps you can implement to foster change in your thought life:

1. Reflect on your most dominate thoughts and determine if these thoughts are in agreement with peace, happiness, honesty, productivity, success and health.

2. Reprogram your thoughts by exposing your mind to words and images that feed your thoughts and properly influence your emotions, conversation, and behavior. Exposing your thoughts to new words and images can be a challenge in and of itself for the simple reason that we are creatures of habit; and when change is a requirement for progress, there can be resistance. Why? Over time your thoughts have developed their own will and perception of how to respond to life by seeking words and images (i.e., people, places, and things) that support what you desire to become. This might mean you may have to let go of friends that share the same old behavior patterns as you do and expose yourself to a totally different set of people and environment that generate positivity.

You can also benefit from seeking counseling from your pastor or therapist to address any nonproductive and irrational thoughts you may be having. Counseling professionals can help you in seeking alternative ways in replacing your negative thoughts with more productive ones. Never let pride stand in the way of your getting help, because you and your child will benefit in the long run.

Every child should be given the opportunity to thrive from a loving, caring, happy, and productive environment, but it all starts from how you, the parent, think and how you decide to present life to your child. Remember, you determine what your child considers; and what your child considers is how she will respond, either good or bad.

3. Become what you are thinking. Now that you have modified your thought life, it is time to put those new thoughts into action by becoming those thoughts through your behavior. For example, if your thoughts consist of being jubilant, then let it show through your facial expressions or let it be heard through laughing. Putting right thoughts into action is not a one-time event but rather a lifelong process that is incorporated into your lifestyle to maintain the existence of your thought life.

Dismissing Negative Thoughts through Words

Teaching your child how to dismiss thoughts that contradict his overall well-being is to his advantage. We spend a lot of time and effort teaching our children at an early age how to get dressed, how to brush their teeth, how to make their bed (some children are still working on this one), how to speak correctly when in the presence of others, and the list of how-tos can go on and on. But how much time do you spend teaching your child how to dismiss unwarranted thoughts that may pose a threat to his happiness, success, and peace?

Let me make something very clear before I proceed any further. I am not saying your child will not experience disappointments in life; nor am I saying your child will never feel sad. But what I am saying is your child definitely does not have to remain in that state of being. Therefore, assist your child in selecting the appropriate words that have the potential of replacing thoughts contradicting their social, mental, physical, or emotional welfare.

The most impactful way to assist your child in dismissing negative thoughts is by staying in touch with her thoughts. Meaning, asking your child what she is thinking about on a daily basis. This will help you monitor if your child's thoughts are on the right track. No child's thoughts should be secret as long as she is under your supervision. There are a lot parents who wished they had explored their child's thoughts when they were younger; they probably would be alive today and not a victim of suicide or other harmful behaviors.

Never let your child think "alone," especially during those sensitive years of his life, but rather explore his thoughts with him so you can assist him in redirecting any thoughts that most likely will not have a favorable outcome. Assisting your child in processing his emotions and feelings rather than letting his emotions and feelings control his behavior is all about properly connecting with his thoughts through conversation and introducing him to words and images that promote a successful, healthy, and peaceful life.

Let's briefly look at four different thought processes a child can be subject to in life:

1) Factual-Detailed Thoughts: Factual-detailed thoughts are based on an individual concentrating on facts or details of an event that just occurred. This form of thought process is actually focusing on what just happened to you or someone else. This type of thinking can also be referred to as surface thinking; what I can see right now.

2) Thoughts That Make It Worse Than What It Is. This type of thought process results from an individual allowing an actual physical event or make-believe event to repeat itself over and over again in their mind. This excessive replay causes the individual to rewrite the script in the canvas of their imagination, making it worse than it is. For example, Chloe and her friend Mary had a little disagreement at school. As a result, the two of them are not talking to each other. Chloe keeps mentally replaying the event that took place at school between Mary and herself to the point that she is now having thoughts about how her peers will no longer be her friend because of what happened. Remember, it just started between herself and Mary; now she has the whole school involved.

3) Wonderland Thoughts. These are thoughts that come out of the woodwork and have no significant meaning to them at all; just the fact that it makes a person wonder where those thoughts came from. Wonderland thoughts are not linked to any particular event or situation, but yet are still powerful enough to make an individual feel like it is a real-life experience if pondered on long enough.

4) Solutions Thoughts. Solutions Thoughts are thoughts in which an individual mentally imagines herself above the situation at hand by seeing or focusing on an image that is better than the current situation. For example, little Ricky was not selected to play on the baseball team this year. Rather than rent space in his mind regarding not making he baseball team, Ricky chooses to visualize himself hitting a home run and being selected on the baseball team. What Ricky is doing is seeing himself playing on the school's baseball team before it becomes a physical reality. Ricky even takes it further by having his parents hire a trainer to assist him in improving his athletics skills, which will make him a stronger candidate for next year's tryouts.

Out of all the thought processes I presented to you, the only thought process your child should permit into the canvas of his imagination is solution thoughts. Why? Solution thoughts are instructional and purpose driven. They also keep an individual, your child, above what the senses or facts say cannot be done.

Assisting your child in processing his emotions and feelings rather than letting his emotions and feelings control his behavior is all about properly connecting with his thoughts through conversation.

This will introduce your child to words and images that will assist him in dismissing thoughts in an effective manner so he can begin to consider thoughts that will have a positive impact on his life.

Steps Toward Purposeful Thinking

This section of this chapter is more of a review than anything else. Why? I have basically presented in detail all of the essential steps (all except delaying time to ponder on or direct one's attention to preselected words and images) that your child needs to have in her arsenal in an effort to operate on a level of purposeful thinking.

Just by your taking time out of your busy schedule to read this section of the book and activating these steps puts your child at an advantage from the standpoint that she is learning at an early age how to discipline her thoughts in order to fruitfully address life situations and events when they pop up unexpectedly. Your child also has an advantage over other children who do not practice purposeful thinking, as a result, limiting their ability to look beyond their current state of being and where they should be (i.e., happy, calm, courageous, productive, healthy, etc.).

That is to say, by properly using purposeful thinking, your child will be prevented from replaying the thoughts associated with the negativity of the situation. Faithfully utilizing these steps towards purposeful thinking and connecting with positive thoughts or images will guide your child on how to appropriately approach the situation despite the opposition it presents. Purposeful thinking is a lifelong process and therefore requires discipline and commitment. With that in mind, here are the following steps:

1. Preselect words and images (i.e., people, places, and things) that are in agreement with the wholeness of one's well-being.

2. Constantly keep the words and images in the forefront of your child's mind until they become what he is solely considering.

3. Delegate quiet time for your child to ponder on the words and images that have been presented for her to be successful in life.

4. Dismiss thoughts that oppose or contradict the wholeness of your child's overall well-being.

5. Replace negative or nonproductive thoughts by speaking words and seeing the image of the words that are being spoken until your mind is back in sync with reality.

Parents, I would like to reiterate before concluding this chapter that it is your responsibility to teach your child how to be conscious of what he is thinking about, because what he is allowed to behold will eventually become his reality.

Chapter 7

EMOTIONAL STABILITY AND SUPPORT

Is it possible for your child to live a life that consists of emotional stability? The answer is yes! Emotional stability is not a special wish that someone makes and hopes will come true one day. Emotional stability is a reality that can exist in the lives of those who put time and effort into making sure their thought life is constantly being exposed to words that create images sturdy enough to keep one's emotions stable rather than scattered everywhere.

Thoughts that are more solid or stable become a dependable driving force of one's emotions as they encounter life's challenges and joyful events. An individual's emotions, in this case your child's, should never be designated as the driver of her emotions because emotions are not designed to be independent of her thoughts. I know this sounds a little bit deep right now, but if you can grasp this information I am about to present to you and consistently apply this information both in your life and your child's life, both of you will have a positive outlook on life with emotions that are stable.

Emotions Are Real

Emotions are real and designed to assist you and me in not only understanding but also feeling the results of the experience in which life presented itself. For example, the loss of a loved one can be both sad and hurtful. An individual's level of understanding of losing a loved one is based on the words (i.e., receiving news regarding the death of a loved one, etc.) or images (i.e., physically viewing the body during a funeral) that were presented and processed within an individual's mind, which activated the emotions most suitable in allowing the individual to relate to the experience of losing a loved one. So in essence, words create thoughts or images and thoughts activate emotions.

Finally, emotions trigger feelings that are expressed through our facial delivery, body language, or opinions—all of which are considered as some form of physical action or behavior. When your child's thought process is unorganized, meaning if she has never been properly trained in taming or governing her thoughts, your child will always be driven by her emotions rather than having the ability to control them. Emotions can be demanding, and it is your responsibility to teach your child how to manage her emotions accordingly.

Maintaining Emotional Stability

Here is a list of helpful suggestions you can use to teach your child how to maintain emotional stability. Once again, this process will not work overnight, but by consistently implementing the following steps, you will have the results you so desire for your child.

1. Quickly respond to your child's negative emotions by exploring and processing the emotions with your child. Then find the positive in the midst of a negative situation and focus on that. What you are doing is teaching your child how to shift his thoughts from the negative to the positive so his emotions with not become the driver, but rather the passenger. Negative emotions that are allowed to linger for a length of time will eventually settle and physically be represented through your child's behavior.

2. Challenge your child (when of age) by playing games that require him to determine which emotions should be kept as a friend, and what emotions should not be considered as a friend, but only a visitor. Meaning, emotions that you and your child refer to be as being a visitor should not be avoided altogether because negative emotions are a part of life (i.e., fear, anger, sadness, etc.). But they should not be the sole emotion that dictates to your child's state of being throughout life.

For example, Melinda is always sad, even when everything around her is joyful and loving. First of all, we need to be emotionally supportive by addressing the issue of why Melinda is sad all the time. Once this has been resolved, we need to assist her in reprogramming her mind by constantly exposing her to words and images (i.e. people, places, and things) that reflect joyfulness. This will produce an environment where positive rather than negative emotions can dominate her state of being. Creative games are an excellent way of teaching your child the appropriateness of her emotions and how to maintain control of them through what she is mentally considering.

3. Assist your child in determining the genuineness of their emotions. You will discover as humans our emotions are constantly changing from one moment to the next as a result of what is being presented to our mind. That is why we should not depend on our emotions to determine the outcome of our day. Our emotions are constantly at work trying to keep up with our thoughts by releasing feelings that rightfully represent their (emotions) existence.

Many times our emotions are "prematurely" activated by a thought that is not real and has no validity for its existence. So how can the emotion be genuine when it is a byproduct of a make-believe thought? For example, your child may feel depressed because she had a thought regarding not having any food to eat, while at the

Reflections

Reflections

HONORING YOUR ROLE AS A PARENT

I believe this chapter of the book represents the whole book in its entirety from the standpoint that how you see yourself as a parent will have a tremendous impact on how you will perform in your role as a parent while loving, nurturing, cultivating, guiding, and protecting your child during the course of parenthood. When you honor your role of being a parent, you are placing high value on the role you have accepted as being the overseer of another person's life.

An overseer manages or supervises those who are under their leadership in order to increase productivity and maintain harmony within the organizational structure. Well, your family is your organizational structure where you oversee the growth and development of your child. In addition, you as an overseer maintain harmony between those who exist within your family unit by creating rules and releasing love that generates a harmonious environment that fosters a healthy transitional experience from childhood to adulthood.

This chapter will cover the following:

1. Reasons why it is important for parents (or caregivers) to honor their role as a parent.
2. How to honor your role as a parent or caregiver.

Reasons for Honoring Your Role as a Parent

I have found that when a person has a clear understanding of the relevance of something, they will value the existence of a thing. For whatever reason, there are a lot of parents out there who do not honor their role as a parent simply because they have never been taught or witnessed their own parent honoring their role as a parent.

In other words, there was no history of a mental "photographic" print (also known as schemas) that represented an individual's memory of his parents honoring their role as a parent. As a result, he may experience difficulty when attempting to make sense of the daily practices, roles, responsibilities, and the establishing of rules related to parenthood simply because no information was stored or organized as it relates to honoring one's role as a parent. So a byproduct of an individual not understanding the importance of honoring one's role as a parent can lead him to abuse his role as a parent rather than cherishing the role in which he was called to fulfill.

The following reasons I am about to present to you are not only the reasons why it is important for a parent to know their role as a parent, but will definitely get you heading in that direction. They will encourage you because you will be on the right path.

Reason #1: Leader

Being a parent automatically places you in a leadership position that requires you to lead your child in the way which is right—socially, emotionally, mentally, physically, and morally. However, to be an effective leader over your flock, you must first know where you are going and what to do once you get there. There is an old saying, "A leader is born, not made." That is true in many cases, but a parent still needs to be open to learning about being an effective parent in order to be an effective leader within in their role as a parent.

Just like a child that is born into royalty, it is predestined they will become the next king or queen once their parents step down from their throne or pass away. But they must be properly taught regarding the role of a king or queen even though royalty is in their blood. A child cannot rule a country at the age of two, but rather must be mentally and physically groomed (i.e. the etiquettes of royalty, etc.) before they are actually ready to operate in their role of a king or queen.

It is all a process. So it is for you. You are born into a family, but you must be mentally and physically groomed through observation, books, parenting classes, or solid teaching from a reliable source on how to be an effective leader over your flock before you actually lead your family.

Reason #2: Protector

You must protect those you are leading to honor your role as a parent. Protect them from what? Anything or anyone that has the potential of interfering with the growth, development, and overall well-being of your child. That is why it is a must that you be sensitive to the following:

1. What your child's eye gate and ear gate are being exposed to on a daily basis.

2. Who you allow to be in the presence of your child, either an adult figure or a child who is the same age or older. I would like to add that not everyone should be allowed to babysit your child.

3. Being sensitive to the level of safety that exists in and out of your home environment. For example, in the

times in which we live, it is not safe for your child to walk alone to and from school.

Reason #3: Nurturer

The third reason why it is important for you to honor your role as a parent is that you are the primary nurturer of your child. Meaning, you are the main source in which your child can depend on to be properly cared for and encouraged during the process of growth and development. Look at it this way; nurturing your child becomes the fuel they need to exist and advance in life.

Reason #4: Provider

Many times when we hear or see the word "provider" we associate it with being the head of the family or participating in meeting the financial obligations pertaining to your particular household. Yes, being a provider does mean you are financially responsible for taking care of your family, but it is not the sum total of being a provider.

A provider in reference to honoring your role as a parent is also based on your providing love, emotional support, protection, encouragement, direction, correction, and wisdom so your child is balanced and not experiencing any form of depletion (i.e., mentally, physically, socially, morally, etc.) that would stagnate their growth and development. Truly honoring your role as a parent by being a provider is not an option but an automatic response.

Reason #5: Cultivator

Another reason why you should place high regards towards your role as a parent is because you are given the unique ability to discern the gifts or talents your child possesses. By discerning the gifts existing in your child, you are responsible for cultivating, or what I call "tending," to the development of that particular gift or talent until it reaches a level of maturity.

A gift or talent that is ripe or seasoned is then ready to be appropriately displayed through your child's physical actions within an arena that accepts, welcomes, and appreciates the existence of the gift or talent. As a parent you are cultivating or tending to your child's attitude, thoughts, motivational drive, intentions (or purpose for doing), and the quality of time in which he invests and protects his talent or gift.

This all contributes to fertilizing the ground of your child's life to fulfill destiny. For example, if your child is gifted in the area of music, singing, or playing an instrument, you would cultivate her musical talent by acquainting her with various styles of music that will reaffirm her musical talent.

How to Honor Your Role as a Parent

Now that you have been given the opportunity to gain a better understanding of the importance of honoring or having a high regard for your role as a parent, let's now entertain the thought by answering the question of how one, the parent, actually honors their role as a parent.

1. Be Cognizant of Your Responsibility - A parent that honors, values, or places high regard towards their role as a parent is not only cognizant of their responsibilities, but also takes responsibility by being diligent in fulfilling the call of duty simply because they are committed to the cause—parenthood. It is the responsibility of parents to set rules and properly establish boundaries for their child to effectively interact within the domain of their family system.

It is the responsibility of the parent to emotionally and socially support their child by demonstrating love towards their child on a daily basis. It is the responsibility of the parent to correct their child when they are acting out of the nature in which they have been taught. The responsibility of being a parent is endless, but the opportunity to share life with another life and see them grown into a responsible and productive adult is priceless.

2. Avoid Self-Centeredness - Once your little one makes his physical appearance into your life, the focus or attention should automatically be off of you and on to the well-being and safety of your child. Priority shifts from singular to plural. Therefore, there is a demand on your time, finances, unconditional love, attention, moral conduct, and social, and emotional support. These are all being deposited into your child's life so he can effectively explore and learn how to adapt to the world in which he lives.

I am not saying to not set aside quiet time for yourself to regroup. Nor am I saying to neglect your physical and mental well-being for the sake of raising your child. What I am saying is that you must constantly be aware it is not solely about you. Why? Your child is not you, but your child is part of you. No more saying, "When I have eaten, the whole household has eaten!" Why? Because there is another mouth waiting to have her pallet and tummy satisfied.

3. Protect Your Role as a Parent - This step requires you to demand, through words and actions, that you are respected as an authority figure in your child's life. Sadly, a lot of parents deny themselves the honor of being respected as a parent because they do not respect themselves. My husband and I were conversing one evening and he said he had watched a talk show where Dr. Phil was interviewing a couple. This particular show was directed towards the husband being physically abusive to his wife and their two-year-old son.

Not only was it bad enough that the son was a witness and victim to domestic violence, but the son was now beginning to emulate this dysfunctional behavior (physical abuse) by hitting his mother in the face. Wow! Like father, like son. The mother had no respect for herself, and as a result she was unable to demand the respect she so deserved from her son. Because of this, her identity not only as a woman but also as a wife and mother was lost in the midst of the domestic violence. So how do you protect your role as a parent?

1. Quickly correct your child when she disrespects you in public and private. In other words, when a child not only disrespects the boundaries you have established for yourself as adult but also the boundaries you have established between the two of you, correction needs to

be made immediately to avoid further damage, A child should never get away with disrespecting you because if she is not corrected the first time, she can easily assume this is how you want to be treated as a parent.

2. Set clear boundaries that separate and clearly define you as being the adult and them as being the child. Never let your child think they are your equal, because they are not. If your child is allowed to think they are your equal, then they will challenge you as an adult. When you feel like your child is stepping over their boundaries, gently remind them that they are the child and they will act accordingly.

3. Make sure your words and actions do not contradict your role as a responsible parent. For example, how can a parent, who is not only heavily addicted to drugs but also is absent from their child's life, expect the child to respect their role as a parent if the parent does not respect their role as a parent themselves? Children are always observing your actions even when you think they are not looking, so make sure you are correctly respecting yourself as a parent.

Reflections

Reflections

KEEPING YOUR WORD

"Your word is your bond" and "You are only as good as your word" are ancient clichés, but let the truth be told, these ancient clichés still hold value in their meaning as they relate to understanding how to effectively operate in life. Let me elucidate this further. There is nothing worse than a parent habitually failing to keep their word, especially when it comes to their child depending on every word that is coated with a promise to be fulfilled.

Oftentimes as parents we have good intentions to do what we said we were going to do, but sometimes we can be easily distracted with life or make a promise without considering all that is entailed in fulfilling that promise. Either way you look at it, from the child's perspective we did not keep our word with them. Granted, children as a whole have a lot of resilience, and as a result are quick to put forgiveness into effect. I don't care how many times a parent messes up, in the eyes of the child the parent can do no wrong simply because the parent is that child's hero.

However, as the child becomes older and more mature, his perception begins to change from seeing his parent as just his parent, but as a person. In other words, the child becomes more observant of the human side of his parent in regards to their strengths and fragilities. The child is beginning to hold his parent accountable for their actions, in addition to keeping record in the memory bank of the times another empty promise was made.

I personally believe and have witnessed to confirm my belief that people who were constantly disappointed by a parent throughout childhood are prone to be less secure, especially when it comes to trusting the words of others. I just mentioned a key word and that word is "trust." Trust is not only a key component, but also what I consider to be a priceless commodity that is released from keeping a promise to another person.

Trust not only develops but also validates an individual's track record, therefore labeling the person as being one who is dependable, reliable, or having the strength or ability to do what needs to be done. When you trust someone, you are resting with assurance rather than reservation. Why am I harping so much on this word trust? For the following reasons:

1. Trust evolves from fulfilled promises; not only a promise of doing something special for your child, but also the promise to provide, love, direct, and protect your child.

2. Trust strengthens the relationship between you and your child.

3. Trust brings your child reassurance and peace as a result of your being committed to keeping your word and also committed to fortifying the social, emotional, and mental constituents of the parent-child relationship. Trust is like the glue that holds the relationship together. Trust is like the water that makes the relationship grow. Finally, trust

is like the harmonic sounds that are released from the voices of a choir; it brings unity to the relationship.

The Lasting Effects of Fulfilled Promises

The lasting effects-sound character, honoring one's word and social and emotional support of fulfilled promises that are manifested in your child's life, are immeasurable and are vital in the development of her interpersonal relationships with others. May I once again reiterate that in this chapter I am not solely referring to but am primarily focusing on keeping your word when you are planning to do something special for your child. But I am also referring to keeping your daily promise of providing, protecting, loving, and guiding your child.

These lasting effects-sound character, honoring one's word and social and emotional support, are what I call positive residues that are deposited into the child's life, formulating his communication and behavioral patterns. Remember, a child's communication and behavioral patterns are learned by the social interactions that are modeled before the child within their home environment. Simply saying, you are teaching your child how to converse and act by your conversations and actions alone.

Modeling is the channel in which your child develops specific communication and behavioral patterns that are stored and organized in their memory bank and eventually used in various situations as they develop interpersonal relationships with others. Let's examine the positive residues or the lasting effects of fulfilled promises individually in order to gain a better insight of the importance of being committed to keeping your word with your child.

Sound Character

The first lasting effect of fulfilled promises is sound character. Did you know by keeping your word you are assisting in creating the makeup of your child's character? Character is what I define as being the mental and principle-driven disposition of an individual. In essence it is one's thoughts towards a matter and the way in which they address the matter, right or wrong, good or evil, which speaks for a person's character. Being consistently committed in fulfilling the promise you made to your child so integrity prevails and becomes the identifiable link to your child's character being sound. Remember, do what's right because it is right is an attribute of sound character.

Honoring Your Word

The second lasting effect of fulfilled promises is that of honoring one's word. Sadly, we live in a society where one's words are not valued like they used to be but are randomly used, therefore becoming a bunch of rhetoric with no significant meaning. In other words, people are oftentimes saying something just for the sake of saying something. That is not good for the simple reason that there are a lot of unfulfilled promises aimlessly wandering in the mind of some child who is patiently waiting for their arrival. But the promise maker failed to take action and fulfill the promise because they do not honor their word.

The lasting effects of keeping your word to your child is that you not only honor the words that come out of your mouth, but your child also respects the words they hear being released from your mouth. Therefore, words are not aimlessly wandering but are purposefully being aimed at achieving a goal—keeping your word. Honoring your word is a beautiful attribute of your character that can be physically witnessed by your child and the example she can mirror in the future. So how do you honor your word?

1. Choose your words carefully; do not release words just to be heard.

2. Make sure the words you speak support who you are. In other words, if your character is sound, then the words you speak are coated with integrity and assurance that what has been said will be done. While on the other

hand, the words that come out of an individual who is known for having a shady character have no truth or substance to bring what is being said to pass; all talk, but no action.

3. Do what you said you were going to do. If you promise your child two dollars for cleaning up his room, then give your child the two dollars he is expecting to receive.

Social and Emotional Security

The third lasting effect of fulfilled promises is the social and emotional security your child carries with her as she engages in life. As I indicated earlier in this chapter, a child constantly exposed to unfulfilled promises becomes socially withdrawn and insecure. This causes her to avoid interacting with others for fear of being disappointed or hurt if that person does not keep their word. Emotional insecurity sets in when the child has never been given an explanation for why the promise was never fulfilled. It also sets in when the child does not receive an apology as a form of acknowledgment to help mend feelings associated with past disappointments.

The lack of emotional support to confirm the negative emotional impact (i.e., anger, sadness, etc.) a child may be experiencing can be contributed to the lack of sensitivity on behalf of the parent not keeping their promise. A child is like a tree that is constantly growing. A tree consistently exposed to the proper amount of sunlight, adequate amounts of water, and nutrients from the soil will grow. Well, the words spoken to and over your child are the sunlight, water, and nutrients your child needs to be socially and emotionally secure both as a child and also as an adult.

How Do I Keep My Word?

There are some basic steps you as the parent can take from now on to make sure your words are not aimlessly wandering when it comes to making and keeping a promise. First of all, make promises you can keep. Realistic promises are more prone to be fulfilled than promises that are unrealistic or normally require too much time, energy, and oftentimes money.

Secondly, if you are unable to keep your promise, then sit down with your child and explain why a particular promise you made will not be fulfilled at this time and apologize accordingly. Do not rush over the fact that you were unable to keep your word like it is no big deal. You are not the one in the expectancy seat; your child is. May I add, there is nothing worse than altogether ignoring the fact that you made a promise. Sweeping everything under the rug like nothing happened sends a message to the child that her feelings are irrelevant, especially when she comes of the age of understanding. Please be sensitive to your child's feelings!

Finally, reschedule another time to fulfill the promise you made and do it. If you find it difficult to fulfill this promise, then let it go and do not let this promise resurface again until you are fully committed mentally, physically, and in some cases financially. It is better not to make a promise at all than to make a promise and not keep it. When you honor your word, your child will do the same.

Reflections

Reflections

Chapter 10

MEANINGFUL CONVERSATION

Being an effective communicator is one of the most powerful tools your child could ever possess in their lifetime. The proper usage of words and having the creative ability to articulate their native language when conversing with others will open doors and answers questions that would otherwise remain closed or unanswered due to an individual's ability to participate in meaningful conversations.

The key to being an effective communicator is valuing the words that come out of your mouth and recognizing the power they carry, then appropriating those words at the right time. Parents, I hope you will sense the urgency of the message I am trying to convey in this chapter and that is, our future generation is being heavily exposed and highly influenced by the unlimited communication capabilities of today's technology to the point that good, old-fashioned verbal communication is becoming secondary rather than primary.

It has become a common observation to see a parent driving and the child (or teenager) in the passenger seat texting away or playing a game on their iPhone rather than engaging in meaningful conversation with their parent. This is a disadvantage because the child's social skills are gradually being stripped. Parents, you should never give consent to any form of technological device to be used as a replacement of verbal communication. Technology should never be considered as your child's primary teacher when it comes to learning the art of meaningful conversation. Words coming from an audible voice can impact the heart and soul whereas technology cannot.

So if you would please squeeze this last essential nugget into your arsenal, you will be good to go. In this chapter I want to challenge you to invest quality time in assisting your child in developing sound communication skills that will allow him to appropriately explore, understand, and pursue the world in which he lives, intelligently. I will be covering the following:

1. What is meaningful conversation?

2. The impact meaningful conversation has on your child's thought process.

3. Establishing meaningful conversation by exploring one's surrounding.

Meaningful Conversation: What Is It?

Meaningful conversation is a dialogue between two or more people that contains what I call a wealth of substance—wisdom, empathy, encouragement, knowledge, humor, and love that is released during the conversation. It will leave a lasting impression on the hearts and minds of those who partook in the meaningful conversation. The purpose of meaningful conversation as it relates to you and your child are the following:

1. To challenge your child to think beyond the norm. Meaningful conversation develops your child's higher

order thinking skills and challenges her to go beyond the facts in order to explore the various possibilities.

2. To assist your child in appropriately and effectively exploring people, places, and things existing within his surroundings and the purpose of their existence.

3. To teach your child how to position himself and make sound decisions when faced with life's challenges.

4. To equip your child with sound communication skills that allow her to develop healthy social and emotional skills.

5. To aid in the enhancement of your child's language development so she can employ words effectively and appropriately while conversing with others and also have a clear understanding when listening to others.

6. To assist your child in adequately expressing his feelings, emotions, wants, or opinions when in a disagreement regarding a particular topic or situation.

7. To teach and encourage your child how to share and receive information.

Meaningful Conversation and the Thought Process

I have already established the fact that your child's thoughts are triggered by words. These words create images in your child's mind which now become the blueprint he uses to gauge his actions towards a certain situation. Right in the midst of a meaningful conversation there is a wealth of substance that stimulates a child's ability to see things with his imagination before it becomes visible to the physical eyes.

So what are you implying, Sheryl? Make sure what you are saying to your child is worth him seeing. For example, if the majority of the conversation you have with your child consists of how hard life is and you have to accept what life deals to you, or you fear this or you fear that, then you have participated in creating an image in your child's mind. This image is that life is too big for him to pursue and conquer. He will believe fear is the solution to avoiding the unknown, rather than pursuing life head on.

The blueprint that exists on the canvas of your child's imagination is a floor plan composed of fear and defeat. You have children just like what I have described, constantly in fear and afraid to go beyond the norm because they do not want to be rejected or labeled as being a failure. This is all due to the fact that their parents chose to have meaningless as opposed to meaningful conversation with their child. It is all about the words you speak!

Meaningful conversation, conversation that contains a wealth of substance, is an excellent way to expand your child's higher order thinking skills. When a child's higher order thinking skills are being properly developed and exercised daily, she welcomes being mentally challenged to think beyond the factual presentations of life. This allows her to explore other possibilities that not only expound upon the facts, but also in some cases dispute the facts. In other words, you are stretching or mentally exercising your child's mind to see the solution as an obtainable possession in her life. If your child can see it, she can have it.

Finally, meaningful conversation establishes response templates that are stored in your child's memory bank and retrieved when displaying a physical action, or what is commonly known as a behavior. Meaningful conversation interjects wisdom and guidance on how a child should conduct herself both in public and private, on a social and an intellectual level.

Growing up as a child, the meaningful conversation my brother and I had with our parents would consist of topics such as being respectful towards our elders. The wealth of substance contained in understanding the importance of valuing and honoring our elders was developed into a response template that was stored in the memory bank of our minds. It was physically displayed and is still being displayed when we are amongst our elders.

Exploring through Meaningful Conversation

Meaningful conversation allows you to explore life with your child. It offers you an opportunity to give your input on what you desire for your child to consider as it pertains to how to live and understand life. By way of explanation, during the midst of meaningful conversation with your child, you are defining life through examples, illustrations, or concrete information that transfer over into his adult years. This serves as an instructional guide on how to operate cogently in society.

So what is required of you to effectively explore life with your child through meaningful conversation? Or, how can you make sure your child is getting the most out of the conversations the two of you have while exploring life? Let's look at the following recommendations:

1. The Right Time, the Right Place. Oh, how we can all attest to the fact that life can be demanding and requires a lot of our attention. Bills, family, work, and the list can go on and on. This can hypnotize us to the point that we neglect to seize the opportune time to help our child understand his surroundings. Always set aside time when it is just you and your child. It may be just going for a walk, drive, visiting a museum, or staying home and baking some cookies. Let this be a time when you and your child can converse with each other without any interruptions.

Conversations should always be exchanged between you and your child, but those right-time, right-place moments are times in which you and your child can go more in depth when exploring and understanding life. During this time, your child may ask a lot questions due to their heightened curiosity, but the special times allocated for exploring life allow you to answer your child's questions accordingly.

2. Acknowledging and Expanding. Not only acknowledging what your child knows, but also helping him to expound on what he knows is an intricate part of meaningful conversation. For example, you and your child are walking in the park and you notice him observing how tall the tree is. He tells you that water helps the tree grow big and strong. You proudly acknowledge his level of understanding in regards to the effect water has on the growth of the tree. So you may expound by asking your child, "By what route does the tree receive the water in order to grow?" You can even take it further by asking him, "Who else or what else needs water to grow and be healthy?" What you are doing is expanding his mind and employing his language skills as he explores in an effort to understand the naturalist side of life.

3. Be Open to Questions. It is important for your child to feel free to ask you questions for the simple fact that life is a big question from a child's perspective. As a result, she is looking to you for the answers to those questions. Three things you must considered when answering the questions your child has for you:

1. Do not rush over the answer. If the question is important enough for your child to ask, then it should be just as important for you to assist you child in finding the answer as the both of you engage in meaningful conversation. A rushed-over answer is simply giving the child a yes or no answer, or giving her the answer to the question without exploring the rationale behind the answer.

2. There should be dialogue going back and forth between you and your child as you assist him in arriving to the answer, as opposed to giving him the answer yourself.

3. All the while you and your child are dialoguing, make sure you are exposing him to new words and the proper usage of those words in order to strengthen his language development skills.

Reflections

Reflections

Closing Words

Throughout this book I have endeavored to challenge you to not only accept but also embrace the fact that your child is your business. As soon as your precious child made her grand entrance into your world, things automatically shifted, and the responsibility for caring for your child socially, physically, mentally, emotionally, morally, and financially took precedence.

It is during this process of raising your child when demands must be attended to before your child's developmental stages can be successfully met. This entails you as a parent to be fully committed in constantly depositing wisdom, love, guidance, instruction, and reassurance to effectively cultivate an image of excellence in the life of your child. This will serve as a blueprint that will navigate your child throughout the course of life.

All that has been presented to you in this book: vertical relationship verses horizontal relationship; the different types of boundaries; meaningful conversation; purposeful thinking; public social grace; voice distinctions; social and emotional impartation; honoring your role as a parent and more; are essential components in creating a structured environment where your child can thrive socially, emotionally, physically, mentally, and morally. I charge you parents to wake up and take your rightful place as the overseer, navigator, protector, carpenter, and gardener of your child's life.

You monitor what you want your child to consider; you model the appropriate social and emotional skills you desire your child to emulate; you make sure your child is loved and protected; you're the one that nourishes words of life into your child's inner image so his image can stand tall and strong; you're the one that corrects your child when she is wrong; you're the one that shows your child how to love and to respect others; you're the one that shares life and laughter with your child; you're the one that recognizes and cultivates the gifts and talents dwelling on the inside of your child; and finally, you are your child's biggest fan and his loudest cheering section. I cannot express it enough; your child is your business, so take pride in what you were destined to do, being a parent.

May peace, love, and courage be with you as you continue down the path of parenthood.

Warmest Regards,
Sheryl L. Brown